YEARNING
MINDS
& BURNING
# HEARTS

Yearning
M I N D S
& Burning
H E A R T S

Rediscovering
the Spirituality
of Jesus

Glandion Carney
and William Long

 Baker Books

A Division of Baker Book House Co
Grand Rapids, Michigan 49516

© 1997 by Glandion Carney and William Long

Published by Baker Books
a division of Baker Book House Company
P.O. Box 6287, Grand Rapids, MI 49516–6287

Printed in the United States of America

Library of Congress Cataloging-in-Publication Data

Carney, Glandion.
    Yearning minds & burning hearts : rediscovering the spirituality of Jesus / Glandion Carney & William Long.
        p. cm.
    Includes bibliographical references.
    ISBN 0-8010-5783-3 (pbk.)
    1. Jesus Christ—Person and offices. 2. Spirituality. I. Long, William Rudolf. 1952–
II. Title.
BT205.C265 1997
232.9'03—dc21   97-33589

Interior art: Dave Wear

For information about academic books, resources for Christian leaders, and all new releases available from Baker Book House, visit our web site:
                                   http://www.bakerbooks.com

CONTENTS

ACKNOWLEDGMENTS

We would like to express special thanks to artist Dave Wear for his sensitive and evocative drawings at the beginning of each part of the book. Dave's work and figures possess, for us, a fine combination of angularity and intimacy, of aloofness and presence, of reflection and engagement. We hope that his work deepens your understanding of the living Jesus.

We also treasure the friendship and professional expertise of Gaily Bos, who acted not simply as a liaison between Dave and us, but enriched the book in countless ways through her meticulous reading of the manuscript, her suggestion of the T. S. Eliot quotations and her spirited encouragement and availability. We wish her well in her budding literary ventures.

Finally, our gratitude would not be complete without mentioning our satisfaction with the quality, friendliness and support of a host of editors and management staff at Baker Book House Company. They were unfailingly helpful to us from the first meeting to discuss our idea in 1996, throughout the stages of the refinement process and to the final production of this book. They have made it a joy for us to be associated with them.

KINDLING
THE FIRE

PART
ONE

STUDYING
JESUS TODAY

INTRODUCTION

GAINING A PERSPECTIVE

Where is the Life we have lost in living?
—T. S. Eliot, *Choruses from "The Rock"*

This book is about Jesus and about us. It is based on the assumption that a study of Jesus' life is the best means of attaining and maintaining personal integrity, harmony, balance and depth in life. The Jesus whom we study is not simply the divine focus of our Sunday worship or a heavenly figure seated at the right hand of God, as the Creeds teach. He is, for us and for the Gospels, a human presence, a spiritual seeker, a wise teacher, a demanding guide and counselor, a healer and a person who sought to be faithful to the requirements of his own discipleship to God.

By studying Jesus' life we discover the rhythms of his own discipleship and the contours of his own spirituality. We meet him as a fellow seeker in the way of faith and as a provider of wisdom, depth and insight for us. Our study of the life of Jesus will make us more grounded in the deep things of life, more able to identify the good amid the competing demands on us, more anchored in integrity and truth, more calm in conflict and more willing to see our lives guided by the hand of a gracious God. It may also, on occasion, bring us confusion and considerable internal struggle as we try to discern how Jesus' conduct and teaching of 2,000 years ago still speaks to us today. In short, by studying the living Jesus, we hope to become better imitators of Jesus, as he was of God.

The Problem

As we approach the end of the twentieth century our lives, as never before, are full of *clutter* and *noise*. Clutter and noise do not happen overnight, but once they have insinuated themselves into our lives, they are almost impossible to eradicate. They intertwine themselves around us, hug us tightly and never let us go. Like tenacious weeds that may grow into the bark of a healthy tree and endanger it, so clutter and noise take root and grow in our lives until they sap us of our spiritual vitality.

Gradually, as we grow older, we accumulate things. We purchase new gadgets and clothes and books, and we discover that we need a larger space to accommodate our goods. What began as a pile on the desk soon becomes a full file cabinet, and then a full closet, and then a full room. Before long we are buried under the weight of accumulated things. Information and possessions that were supposed to set us free are now inundating us. In frustration, we pray, "Save me, O God, for the waters have come up to my neck." (Ps. 69:1)

Clutter not only fills our rooms; it weighs us down. We bow under the load of our possessions like a figure out of Dante's *Inferno*. Our bodies sag as our possessions increase, and we lose the light step and the carefree skip of an earlier age. But, even more significant than the *physical* clutter of our lives is our *spiritual* clutter or *psychological accumulation*. Our physical clutter is only a sign, a demonstration, that reflects the spiritual load we bear. We carry massive loads of guilt with us—guilt for not spending enough time with children, guilt for not caring for aging parents as we ought, guilt for lack of faithfulness and constancy toward a spouse. The weight of the burden increases from a need for forgiveness, dreams deferred and abandoned, injuries inflicted and suffered, abuse experienced, bad choices, and sadness piled upon sadness. The load of our spiritual clutter exceeds that of our physical accumulation. It takes away our springy step and jovial greeting; it can diminish the joy of living.

Then there is the *noise* of our lives which consists of all the clamor arising from the choices that are constantly put before us, calling for our recognition and our decisions, and the resulting belief that our lives will be better because we have more things from which to choose. Our economic system may be the best in the world for providing a high standard of living for its people, but it also exacts a cost from those who participate in it. We think we must listen to all the noise around us if we are to be "wise" participants in our society. The noise of our culture is primarily the siren call of consumption designed to create dissatisfaction with our current life situation. Its simple message to us is: unless you have more, your life cannot be happy. The noise of our culture tries to convince us that we are what we have, what we buy.

Noise and clutter, like ravenous twins, feed upon each other. The noise tells us how inadequate our lives are. So, we purchase and accumulate, in order to become adequate and happy. But the accumulation only produces clutter which, in turn, creates a sense of unease and unhappiness. We ignore the message by listening to the noise again, which assures us that if we just get just one more thing, our lives will be full. Each time the cycle repeats, we are left with emptiness, aimlessness and a vague sense that we are not well.

The results of the clutter and noise are the *loss of integrity and hardness of heart.* The root meaning of the word *integrity* is wholeness or completeness. An integer, in mathematics, is a whole number and can be contrasted with a fraction, a "broken" number. A person of integrity has a deep sense of wholeness and fullness. Our culture falsely claims that this integrity will come only through accumulation and economic capacity, an insidious contention. The very things which culture touts as sources of integrity result in loss of integrity. We have become complex, not simple; torn, not mended; conflicted, not resolved; fractured, not whole. If our possessions could bring integrity, more of us would be people of integrity by now. But they do not, and our ceaseless quest for more shows our spiritual poverty and our lack of wholeness.

Noise and clutter also bring a hardness and coldness of heart. They have an insatiable appetite and demand to be fed. They require us to go out and satisfy them. We must go now, and we must go quickly. We must not delay. So, dutiful servants that we are, we fulfill their bidding. We neglect other important things, and we heed the call of clutter and noise. Our ears learn not to hear the cries of pain all around us; our eyes soon learn not to see the brokenness of our world. All our senses are directed toward the demanding duo of clutter and noise.

Our hearts grow cold to the needs of humanity and to the words of the living Jesus. We avoid hearing the most plain and obvious texts of Scripture and we, like the foolish man of Luke 12, tear down our barns to build bigger ones to accommodate all our possessions. Images of pain flash across the television screen, but before they can register, we "surf" to three or four other stations. Our hearts become hardened and cold, and we become exemplars of superficial living. We need someone to take away the hardness of the heart, to restore our integrity, to remove the plaque that fills our mouths and the impurities that clog our arteries. We need to hear the living Jesus again.

Our Aims

The two central premises of this book are (1) that Jesus, as a Jew living 2,000 years ago, needed to cultivate his own discipleship and deepen his own understanding of God, the world and his task in life, and (2) that by studying Jesus' discipleship, we too become partakers of the depths of the life he lived. We affirm with Christians of all ages that Jesus was "very God of very God," but we also believe in his full humanity. He is like a perfect rose, with all of its petals intact and colorful, but which opens and spreads out as it receives rain and sun. So Jesus' perfection is not inconsistent with his development. His perfection is not a static, but a dynamic reality. It is perfection in action, perfection that grows, perfection that deepens. He, too, needed God. He needed the assurance of God's presence and care. He needed the rhythms of rest and work. He needed to grow and learn, through acceptance and through rejection, through victory and suffering. He is a model for us, today, who need the same things.

To be more specific, on three occasions in this book we will try to show how Jesus grew in his understanding of faith and his mission in life. When we study the call of Jesus, our major point will be that it was far from clear to him at the outset of his public ministry what it meant when God's Spirit descended upon him and he heard the words, "You are my Son, the Beloved; with you I am well pleased" (Luke 3:22). We will also show how it only gradually dawned on Jesus that his mission in life was to die in Jerusalem as the servant of God. Finally, in our consideration of the suffering of Jesus we will suggest that one reason Jesus' disciples and hearers misunderstood him is because there is, at points, a fundamental ambiguity in Jesus' words.

We will see that Jesus' struggle to live a life faithful to God was often fraught with ambiguity and laced with uncertainty. However, there is enough clarity and focus to his life to kindle our hearts and direct our own Christian discipleship. For example, we will show how Jesus' mastery of Scripture not only was more profound than that of his contemporaries, but also helped him understand the rhythms of his life and the work of God through him.

Jesus' mastery of the Scriptures should inspire us to cultivate our knowledge of Scripture and to realize in humility how fickle, impartial and unsteady are our own attempts at mastery.

His life of prayer, we will show, was the key to his ability to read and weigh the hearts of people. Prayer was essential to his ability to heal. A close study of Jesus' life of prayer might lead us to new levels of perception, and through our study of Jesus we too may develop some hidden capacities of spiritual perception we never knew we had.

We have been challenged by Jesus' unwavering commitment to his understanding of his call and his willingness to court unpopularity in order to be true to his mission in life.

We have discovered, through our study, a Jesus who is tremendously accessible to us and speaks to us with great forcefulness yet whose assumptions are so different from those of

Western culture as to make him nearly unrecognizable by contemporary westerners.

Most of all, we have discovered a Jesus who is a dominant person in human history. He is earnest and insightful, reflective and active, patient yet impatient, aggressive yet cautious, demanding yet caring. He remains one of the most compelling teachers and personalities in history. We would like you to share some of the excitement we have felt in our own rediscovery of Jesus through the writing of this book. We invite you to study him, to "learn from him" (cf. Matt. 11:28–29).

By studying his life, we imbibe his spirit. We see him alone before God, in public teaching sessions, in controversy, confronting the injustices and evils of life, with his disciples, abandoned by nearly everyone. He teaches us by specific instruction as well as by example. We learn by observing him and by listening to the nuances of the biblical text. He, as the Good Shepherd, leads us in the way of righteousness by helping us understand, affirm and practice the central principles of life. By his openness to God, we are encouraged to open our hearts to God again. By his ambivalence toward the Law of Moses, we are challenged to reexamine our basic commitments in life. By his steadiness, calmness and courage we are inspired and challenged to exemplify integrity and courage today.

As the title of this book indicates, we will be speaking of the spirituality of Jesus. In many instances, when authors speak of spirituality, they mean the cultivation of the "inner life" and the disciplines that go with it—prayer, study of Scripture, journaling, worship, solitude. But in this book, we want to extend the definition to include other aspects of Jesus' life. His spirit shone through in his times of retreat and engagement, in the quiet as well as the noise of life. Since Jesus taught that the abundance of the heart leads us to speak and to act (Luke 6:45), all of his life can be said to flow from his heart, from his spirit, from his spirituality. We rediscover his spirituality by rediscovering his life.

1

THE PREPARATION

> . . . These are only hints and guesses, Hints followed by
> guesses; and the rest Is prayer, observance, discipline, thought
> and action. The hint half guessed, the gift half understood,
> is Incarnation
>
> —T. S. Eliot, *Four Quartets*

Of making many books there is no end." So say the Scriptures (Eccles. 12:12). Even a cursory survey of the literature about Jesus of the last decade might lead one to revise this scriptural observation: "Of the making of books about Jesus there is no end." Jesus continues to fascinate and allure, nearly 2,000 years after he lived and died in a remote corner of the earth. Part of the reason for his continued appeal is the abiding conviction in Western culture, and American culture specifically, that Jesus has crucial wisdom to impart to us in our day.

At the turn of the twenty-first century we have an ill-defined but real feeling that we have gained the whole world but have lost our souls, and that we cannot afford to abandon our inner life any longer. There is a longing, a yearning, a hunger in our culture for a fuller spiritual life, a life that all the material promises of a wealthy society cannot provide. There is a genuine desire to learn the things of the spirit from a tested and true master. In this context, Jesus retains his appeal. He is bigger than the movement he spawned (Christianity), more accessible and less burdened with tradition than the church, more engaging than any human institution can be. Somehow we feel that if we rediscover Jesus, we can relearn some of the basic lessons of life and faith, the building blocks upon which we can build the new structure of our lives, lives more humane and centered on the deep values which Jesus teaches and embodies.

Jesus continues to call and invite us to study him, to learn of him, to see how his life and spirit can shape ours in the hectic world of the late twentieth century. To that end, several dozen books on Jesus and spirituality have appeared during the last decade. Many of the books are written from a scholarly perspective and seek primarily to present Jesus in the context of the first-century world of Judaism. A good number of new books also probe the subject of spirituality and the nature of the spiritual life, yet they pay little attention to how the person of Jesus helps to shape one's own spiritual pilgrimage. There is a need, which I have tried to supply in this book, for a work that brings together a study of the historical Jesus with the burgeoning contemporary interest in spirituality in order to provide practical, yet thought-provoking, guidance to those seeking to deepen their spiritual lives.

In this chapter I will do three things. First, I will examine the way Jesus is being studied in contemporary popular and scholarly writing in order to position this book in the current debate and conversation. To do this, I will discuss some of the history and goals of the scholarly "quest of the historical Jesus." Some readers might find my brief historical review of this "quest" a bit forbidding. I hope not. I have decided to include it because I think it important to provide a broader context to understand why there is so much interest in Jesus today from a scholarly perspective.

Second, I will briefly discuss the issue of spirituality, introduce some of the authors who are writing significant works on the subject, and justify my approach to the spirituality of Jesus. Third, I want to provide an extended biblical reflection on the passage which provides the title for this book

(Luke 24:13–35). My hope is that the reflection on that passage will provide a helpful stimulus not simply to kindle the fire which the first disciples felt, but also to stimulate us to go further with Jesus, to enter into his inner and outer life, and to discover how his life might shape our lives today. This chapter will conclude with a meditation on John 8, and will emphasize that the life of discipleship is one that begins with passion, but must be carried on with patient love and discipline.

The Preparation—Jesus in the News Today

There is perhaps no person in history whose life has been studied more thoroughly than Jesus. He is the subject of countless weekly Bible studies as well as detailed scholarly portraits. So extensive is the study of Jesus that often a 400-page doctoral dissertation on Jesus or the Gospels will confine itself to one healing story, one parable or even one verse. Since the mid-1980s the steady *flow* of books and articles on Jesus has turned into a *flood*. Even the popular media have picked up on this interest. For example, the 1996 Easter-week cover stories of *Time, Newsweek,* and *U.S. News and World Report* were all about the modern "quest of the historical Jesus" and its effects on Christian faith today. I do not intend this book to be a contribution to that quest, and I disagree with the methods of the "questers" in some significant ways. Nevertheless, I need to take some time to clarify what that quest is and how my effort to rediscover Jesus is indebted to them, yet differs in emphasis and conclusion.

Albert Schweitzer, the great missionary doctor and biblical scholar, coined the phrase, the "quest of the historical Jesus," to describe the effort, mainly by nineteenth-century German scholars, to write about the life of Christ. These scholars were influenced by the critical spirit of historical investigation emerging from the Enlightenment of the eighteenth century. Guided by that spirit, many nineteenth-

19

century German biblical scholars concluded that much of the material in the Gospels did not reflect the real life of the historical Jesus but, rather, the controversies of the emerging church at the end of the first century A.D. The "quest of the historical Jesus" was the attempt to weigh the individual stories in the Gospels to determine which ones, in all probability, could be used for reconstructing a historical-critical life of Jesus. The first phase of the quest lasted from about 1835 to 1914.

Scholars and traditional Christians in England and the United States were, in large measure, offended by the phrase and the quest, and dryly suggested that Jesus was never lost and really needed no rediscovering! Yet, as the nineteenth century wore on, many English-speaking scholars were also joining the quest, adopting the methods and the results of German scholarship.

The time between the World Wars saw the waning of interest in the scholarly quest of the historical Jesus. The leading New Testament scholar of the period, Rudolf Bultmann, doubted if the Gospels gave us anything more than the "echo" of Jesus' voice. Yet, in the early 1950s, some of Bultmann's students called for a new quest of the historical Jesus. These scholars developed a complex array of methods which supposedly helped them separate authentic from non-authentic sayings and stories of Jesus (discussed briefly below), and they were more confident than Bultmann that the actual details of Jesus' life and message could be fairly accurately described.

Scholars differ whether we are still in the "second quest" of the historical Jesus or the third. In any case, the attempt to write a critical life of Jesus is now an international movement, and all New Testament scholars in colleges, universities and seminaries have been affected by the quest to a lesser or greater degree. The significant scholars in the "Jesus Seminar," a decade-long effort among American biblical scholars to reconstruct the life of Jesus according to the most modern scholarly methods, were all steeped in the German historical method. Many of them were students of the leaders of the "second quest" and occupy significant university positions in biblical studies throughout American universities and divinity schools. Several of them maintain a vibrant Christian faith. Others, admittedly, have been badly burned by various expressions of Christian faith and take pleasure in debunking the beliefs of a large segment of the American Christian public. I would like to discuss briefly some of the perspectives established by the "questers," and then show how the emphasis of my work differs from theirs.

The "quest of the historical Jesus" is based upon certain perspectives or "facts" of scholarship. The first one which shapes the "questers'" understanding of the Gospels is that the Four Gospels were probably written between A.D. 70–90. No hard evidence proves this, and many scholars are starting to contest these dates, but at this juncture, this is a "scholarly consensus." That means there were 40 to 60 years between the death of Jesus and the writing of the Gospels. Certainly Christians told stories of Jesus in that intervening period and some accounts of his teaching, miracles or death may have been written during that time, but we have no documentary evidence from that period which survives today.

The second "fact" of modern Gospel scholarship is that as the stories of Jesus were retold and put in writing, they were embellished or changed by the Gospel writers in minor or major ways. The assertion is that the actual stories we have in the Gospels may not be accurate descriptions of what actually happened in the life of Jesus. The narratives were influenced by 40 or more years of retelling, by the faith of the earliest Christian communities, and by the need to apply the stories more explicitly to the needs of the contemporary church. Therefore, the assumption of modern biblical scholars is that there are "layers" of material in the Gospels. Three "layers" are usually identified as follows: that of Jesus (called the "historical" Jesus), that of the earliest Christian community (from about A.D. 30–70) and that of the time of the writing of the Gospels (between A.D. 70–90).

The central question for scholars involved in this quest has been to try to develop "tests of authenticity" to determine which sayings, events and healings attributed to Jesus in the Gospels were produced at the various "layers" of the Gospel tradition. Ultimately, their desire is to determine which of these sayings, events and healings with all likelihood go back to Jesus himself. The tests of authenticity are quite complex and disputed. Scholars do not even agree on what these tests are. A limited discussion of even the most popular ones, such as the tests of distinctness, multiple attestation and coherence, is beyond the scope of this book.

Yet the questions that the Gospel scholar or quester asks of each text are: "Does this teaching or event, in all probability, go back to Jesus? Is the narrative strongly shaped by the early church? Does it appear to be something that the Gospel writer either invented or got from a special source known only to him?" The questions are even more complex than this because many scholars would assert that several Gospel stories may have originated with Jesus but were embellished, added to or otherwise "clarified" at each subsequent stage of the Gospel tradition. So when one reads a scholarly commentary on a Gospel, evangelical or liberal, the scholar will usually try to "disentangle" the various layers of the Gospel tradition. The goal of all of this work is, in the first instance, to hear the voice of the Jesus who lived and died in Palestine around A.D. 30, or in other words, to discover the "historical Jesus."

As I mentioned above, many participants in the modern "quest of the historical Jesus" are people of faith. Their goal is to expose the "bedrock" of the Gospel tradition so that the historical Jesus can speak directly to the church today. They seek to separate Jesus from encrusting church doctrine and hear his unalloyed, pure voice and his call to discipleship today.

In my judgment, however, the modern quest of the historical Jesus is misguided for two reasons. First, the attempt to establish layers of the Gospel tradition, though laudable at points, becomes hopelessly mired in subjectivism. Developing tests for the authenticity of Jesus' words is almost always an exercise in circular reasoning. One begins with a certain picture of who the historical Jesus *must have been* and then develops tests that yield a Jesus who is similar or identical to the one perceived originally. One example of this thinking will clarify my point.

For most of the twentieth century, until around 1980, the dominant image of Jesus in the scholarly literature was as an "eschatological prophet." That means that Jesus believed in and taught the imminent coming of the kingdom of God and the end of the age. It was this notion that was used to explain Jesus' imagery in his parables, the language of his teaching, the urgency of his actions. He had to make haste because of the immediate coming of the kingdom of God and the end times. The scholarly picture which trickled down to the pew through sermons and Bible study classes led by seminary-educated pastors was that Jesus was a proclaimer of the imminent coming of the end times and the kingdom of God.

But in the last few years, scholarly fashions have been changing. More and more scholars are suggesting, and a new "scholarly consensus" may develop by the year 2000, that Jesus really *wasn't* an eschatological prophet after all, but that the imminent expectation of the end of the world was a belief of the early church (from about A.D. 30–70). In fact, modern scholars argue, Jesus may have been more akin to Jewish miracle workers, of whom we have records, or Greek philosophers who spoke in pithy maxims, than to an eschatological prophet. The winds change direction and so does the scholarly "consensus" on the historical Jesus. We probably are no closer to knowing whether any of the suggested pictures is an accurate reflection of Jesus, but the consensus surely provides fertile ground for imaginative speculation, scholarly ingenuity, many Ph.D. dissertations and articles in scholarly journals. It is, in truth, something of a game whose rules change rather frequently.

The second reason why the modern "quest of the historical Jesus" is misguided is because there is no indication in the Gospels or in traditional Christian faith that Jesus is anything other than what he is portrayed in the *entire Gospel tradition*. The Jesus of Christian faith is the Jesus of the Gospels. *All* of the Gospels. The *whole* of *all* of the Gospels.

Were there two cleansings of the Temple by Jesus, or one? Did Jesus meet one or two blind men coming into Jerusalem? Various Gospel writers seem to differ on the details. Whether any particular incident happened exactly as described or may have been refracted through the eyes of faith is really an irrelevant distinction for the Gospel writers and for traditional Christian faith. Do we believe, then, that the Gospel authors may have shaped their materials for their own needs? Certainly. Do the Gospel authors have their own perspectives on Jesus as they tell their stories? Undoubtedly. Does the fact that, for example, the Gospels of Mark and John portray Jesus in different ways, performing different activities, mean that one of them is telling the truth and the other is false, or that both are false? Of course not. Each of the portraits of Jesus in the Gospels is a true picture of him.

We thus have four true pictures of Jesus. But we have one Jesus. How can this be? The best way to explain it, I believe, is through the modern analogy of photography. Many people like to have their pictures taken, but most of us are aware that we have our "good side," or, at least, that we look different when seen from different angles. Pictures that catch us in different poses, dressed in different outfits and engaged in different activities are all true pictures of us, regardless of the fact that we might not even be recognizable from one to the next. Such is the case with Jesus and the Gospels. Each gives us a different "angle" or "snapshot" of Jesus. Each is a true picture, but not a complete picture. It captures an "angle" on Jesus from which we can learn a lot about him, and maybe about the author. But to cut away at the picture, to try to eliminate some features of it because they are not "genuine," is like cutting away at the pictures taken of us because they do not represent the true "us." Once you start cutting, you might as well deface the entire picture!

So, in these two ways, the modern "quest of the historical Jesus" gets us no closer to the Jesus of Christian faith, the Jesus who calls us to discipleship today.

The Preparation—The Study of Spirituality

In this book, I seek the living Jesus but I study him differently from the way many contemporary scholars study Jesus. I seek the *whole* Jesus in *all four* Gospels. I am also interested in the subject of spirituality, but, again, I will define spirituality in a way that is slightly different from most contemporary writers. In the next few pages I will discuss this second preparatory issue, and try to show how my work depends on but differs from much of the modern scholarship on spirituality.

For about twenty years, there has been a strong emphasis in American Protestantism on what is called "spiritual formation." Its older cousin, usually called "discipleship," is familiar to many Protestant Christians, but the contemporary interest in spiritual formation seeks to reconnect with the great history of spirituality in the entire Christian tradition. The best quick definition of "spiritual formation" or "spirituality" is "the increasing vitality and sway of God's spirit in us" (Marjorie Thompson, *Soul Feast,* Westminster John Knox, 1995, p. 6). The modern movement of "spiritual formation" or "spirituality" seeks to be historical in its method and practical in its insights. Its goal is to recapture the historic disciplines of the spiritual life and determine how they might be applied and practiced in our complex and fast-paced modern society.

The search for spirituality is part of a larger movement in Protestantism (which includes ecumenical dialogue and liturgical renewal) to make use of the doctrine, practice and history of the Catholic tradition to enrich our own practice. As Protestants, and evangelical Protestants in particular, have increasingly sought depth in the *experience* of faith rather than simply in the exposition of Christian *doctrine or truth*, we have turned to the huge tradition of Catholic spirituality for help. Those interested in spiritual formation have probed Augustine, Hildegard, the Rhineland Mystics, the Spanish Carmelites, the English Medieval spiritual writers, Medieval Franciscans and Dominicans, the ancient Cappadocian Fathers and a host of other people whose names are not only unfamiliar but also very difficult to pronounce!

Some names connected with this renewed interest among Protestants are Henri Nouwen, Dallas Willard, Richard Foster, Howard Rice and Marjorie Thompson. A good example of a recent book on spirituality by a Protestant writer is *Soul Feast* by Presbyterian minister Marjorie Thompson. She discusses the spiritual yearning of our time, the spiritual reading of Scripture, prayer, worship, fasting, self-awareness and confession, spiritual direction, hospitality and the development of a rule of life. The last topic refers to a challenge she gives contemporary Christians: to develop, in the tradition of the Benedictine or Augustinian Rule, a "canon" or "rule" of life so that our lives will not simply be "informed" by faith but will also be "formed" by it. Her book, she says, is meant to be used and not simply read. In addition to her expositions on these nine topics, she provides quotations from spiritual writers, exercises and practical counsel on how to make the spiritual disciplines powerful in our lives today.

I am indebted to the work on spiritual formation and spirituality but this book will differ in two important ways. First, my emphasis is not on the *practices* of the spiritual life, but on the *person* of Jesus. I am certainly not opposed to the development of spiritual disciplines, but my focus will be on following the contours of the biblical text and meeting a living person, Jesus, who confronts us in all of our sin and glory. Jesus is still, I believe, the most compelling person in history. To seek to follow the movements of his life and to understand how his faith was shaped in the crucible of his life is a task of great urgency for us.

Second, my approach in this book seeks to be more holistic, that is, to look at spirituality as living faithfully in all dimensions of existence. With the possible exception of Richard Foster, the modern emphasis on spirituality concerns primarily the development of what may be called the "inner life." Certainly that is important, and I devote several chapters to those concerns. But when all is said and done, writings which encourage the development of the spiritual life by focusing on the personal or "church-centered" disciplines seem to perpetuate the myth that spirituality is best done in orderly, peaceful or retreat-like situations. Certainly, we need the quiet times of thought and reflection where the soul can drink deeply from the fresh waters of Scripture and where the heart can attune itself again to the realities of the living God. But this is not the whole of the spiritual life.

My emphasis in this book, especially the second half, is on the daily realities of grief, pain, suffering, social injustice and conflict and how Jesus dealt with them. These things are so real, so present and so all-encompassing for so many people that we need to study them and learn how the living Jesus dealt with them. We need to see, for example, how his treatment of a woman with a hemorrhage of blood for twelve years was intimately connected to his ability to develop and maintain his own spiritual awareness and integrity. By studying the source of Jesus' spiritual power as he met the pain and twisted existence of people in the world, we become capable of cultivating our own spiritual power and awareness. By noting how Jesus both provoked and resolved conflicts, we are able to tolerate and manage conflict in our lives. By learning how Jesus dealt with social injustice, we are chastened by the coldness of our commitment to justice in the world and stimulated to reconsider the ethical mandate at the heart of the Gospel. Thus, in this book, we are interested in how Jesus, the whole Jesus of all the Gospels, might shape our understanding of the "inner" and the "outer" life of faith, the life of the spirit and the life in society.

An Invitation—Yearning Minds and Burning Hearts

So we come to the title of the book. It is taken from the incident described in Luke 24:13–35, where two disciples were walking down the road from Jerusalem to Emmaus on the day that Jesus rose from the dead. The story is one that deserves a moment of reflection, for it contains the dynamics of the spiritual life that we and the original disciples need to face.

First there is a *problem* (verses 13–24) that occupies the disciples' minds.

Now on that same day two of them were going to a village called Emmaus, about seven miles from Jerusalem, and talking with each other about all these things that had happened. While they were talking and discussing, Jesus himself came near and went with them, but their eyes were kept from recognizing him. And he said to them, "What are you discussing with each other while you walk along?" They stood still, looking sad. Then one of them, whose name was Cleopas, answered him, "Are you the only stranger in Jerusalem who does not know the things that have taken place there in these days?" He asked them, "What things?" They replied, "The things about Jesus of Nazareth, who was a prophet mighty in deed and word before God and all the people, and how our chief priests and leaders handed him over to be condemned to death and crucified him. But we had hoped that he was the one to redeem Israel. Yes, and besides all this, it is now the third day since these things took place. Moreover, some women of our group astounded us. They were at the tomb early this morning, and when they did not find his body there, they came back and told us that they had indeed seen a vision of angels who said that he was alive. Some of those who were with us went to the tomb and found it just as the women had said; but they did not see him."

The problem, in its barest description, was that the events of the previous few days just didn't "add up" in the minds of these two disciples. They had believed that Jesus would redeem Israel. That belief was apparently dashed by his crucifixion on Friday. But on Sunday a report circulated that Jesus was no longer dead, that some women had seen a "vision of angels" and that the tomb of Jesus was empty. The disciples did not know what to think. Their hopes had been raised, crushed, and partially raised again. Confusion reigned.

Jesus met them in their confusion. They didn't recognize him because "their eyes were kept from recognizing him." Jesus met them in their need, but the cares of the world and concern for their condition had grown up like thorns around them and choked the word of Christ (cf. Matt. 13:22). Jesus tried to draw them out, to explain the situation for them, to give them a chance to express their hope, but the disciples could only speak in the past tense.

The saddest word in this passage is translated, "We had hoped" (verse 21). It is three words in English but only one in Greek, and is in what is called the imperfect tense. In Greek, the imperfect tense describes an action that started, continued and ended sometime in the past. It is best translated, "We were hoping for a while" that he was the one to redeem Israel. The two disciples are awash in their hopelessness, and they don't want the stranger (Jesus) to confuse them further. Our confusion and hopelessness today, in the face of bewildering choices and uncertainties, is little different than that faced by these two men.

Second, there is the word from the *prophets* which Jesus brings (verses 25–27).

Then he said to them, "Oh, how foolish you are, and how slow of heart to believe all that the prophets have declared! Was it not necessary that the Messiah should suffer these things and then enter into his glory?" Then beginning with

Moses and all the prophets, he interpreted to them the things about himself in all the scriptures.

Perhaps because of the abject hopelessness expressed by the disciples in verse 21, Jesus is very direct with them in verse 25. He says, "Oh, how foolish you are, and how slow of heart to believe all that the prophets have declared!" It is reminiscent of another impatient outburst of Jesus when, after his exhilarating experience on the Mount of Transfiguration, he returns to his incompetent disciples and blurts out, "You faithless generation, how much longer must I be among you?" (Mark 9:19). We are now taught that good teachers are not supposed to become angry with their students. Jesus didn't seem to agree.

But after being a bit rough with his two confused disciples, Jesus patiently turned to their needs. He gave them a tour of the Scriptures. Beginning with the law of Moses and continuing through the Prophets and the Writings, Jesus pointed out Scriptures confirming that the events in Jerusalem during the last few days had been foretold. When his disciples were troubled, Jesus pointed them to himself and the words about himself in the Old Testament. His mild exasperation was replaced by great patience as he shared with them the deep things of the Scriptures.

Third, there is Jesus' *presence* with the disciples during a meal (verses 28–31).

> As they came near the village to which they were going, he walked ahead as if he were going on. But they urged him strongly, saying, "Stay with us, because it is almost evening and the day is now nearly over." So he went in to stay with them. When he was at the table with them, he took bread, blessed and broke it, and gave it to them. Then their eyes were opened, and they recognized him; and he vanished from their sight.

Something about Jesus' explanation of the Scriptures touched Cleopas and his friend deeply, and motivated them to invite

Jesus to dinner. Actually, the word *invite* is much too weak. The *Revised Standard Version* translation is, "they constrained him," and the *New International Version* says, "they urged him strongly." Actually, a literal translation would be, "they compelled him by force" to go with them. Some kind of conviction, some kind of longing, some kind of fire had already been kindled in their breasts, and they, literally, would not let go of Jesus.

The meal itself is memorable. It recalls the Last Supper, celebrated with Jesus' twelve disciples just a few days before, in which Jesus gave thanks, took bread, broke it and distributed it to them. When combined with the scriptural explanation on the road, this meal should have left no doubts in the minds of these two men that the living Jesus was with them. Jesus was in the Scripture, he was in the meal, he was in their presence.

The combination of the Scripture and the meal, the Bible and sacrament, opened their eyes (verse 31). They recognized him. The burning in their hearts, lit by the Scriptures, became an open blaze.

The moment of recognition can be one of the most poignant moments in literature or art. Consider Oedipus in Sophocles' tragic *Oedipus the King* who, at the moment of recognition that he would kill his father and marry his mother, blinded himself with a furious intensity. He had seen all of life that he wanted to see. Consider a famous Attic (ancient Greek) vase painting, in which the Greek hero Achilles is shown driving his sword into the breasts of Penthesilea, the queen of the Amazons. At the moment of killing the eyes of the two young warriors meet and they fall in love. The moment of recognition is the moment, also, of death and separation.

In the Gospel of Luke, the moment of recognition for the two disciples is a moment of life. The tragedy of the Greek vase painting and of Sophocles is contrasted by the "comedy" of Luke. The pain of loss in Greek antiquity is now answered by the joy of finding in the Gospel of Christ. As the men recognized Jesus it all came together. Love and joy mingled. And then Christ disappeared, but they didn't need his physical presence any longer. Christ had given them more than enough to think about.

Fourth, there is the *passion* in the disciples after the recognition (verse 32).

> They said to each other, "Were not our hearts burning within us while he was talking to us on the road, while he was opening the scriptures to us?"

The moment of recognition kindled a flame in their cold hearts and removed the cobwebs from their brains. The solution to a great problem unleashed a great passion. Note that the appeal to the disciples was to their heads *and* to their hearts. The Scriptures pried open their minds, which had been unable to assimilate so much confusing data, and the meal opened their hearts and their eyes to see Jesus. The moment of recognition transmuted into a dynamic passion.

The movements of recognition and passion are reminiscent of Alex Haley's wonderful book *Roots* and the 1977 television miniseries based on that book. In tracing his family roots, Haley (played in the last episode by James Earl Jones) could go as far back as his eighteenth-century slave forebears in this country. But then he was stymied. Kunta Kinte, the African from whom he descended had, like most slaves taken from Africa, lost all knowledge of his past in the "Middle Passage" between Africa and America. Could Haley possibly connect his slave past with a specific location in Africa? After tireless research and extensive travel, Haley found the group from which Kunta Kinte had been taken on the banks of the Gambia River. The tribal elder had memorized the genealogy of the tribe for hundreds of years, and intoned in a dry monotone that Kunta Kinte had disappeared in the bush and had been taken away. When he heard this, Jones said with tremendous passion, "Kunta Kinte, I have found you!" This discovery was the key to the documentary, the missing puzzle piece which made Haley's entire family history come together. With this insight, Haley's heart burned within, and that intensity and burning was communicated to every viewer.

Finally, there is the *proclamation* of the disciples (verses 33–35).

> That same hour they got up and returned to Jerusalem; and they found the eleven and their companions gathered together. They were saying, "The Lord has risen indeed, and he has appeared to Simon!" Then they told what had happened on the road, and how he had been known to them in the breaking of the bread.

The two men rose up in that very same hour and returned to Jerusalem with their story. It was an experience that they just had to communicate. Their proclamation, however, had to await that of the other disciples, who greeted them with the statement, "The Lord has risen indeed, and he has appeared to Simon!" Story was added to story, and the church was born.

This story leaves us with some searching personal questions. Do our hearts still burn when we recognize the living Jesus in our midst? What is preventing us from seeing him? What are the cares that need to be removed, or reinterpreted, that prevent us from recognizing him now? Can our minds still yearn to make the truth of Jesus *our* truth? Have the gusty winds of life so cooled our ardor and frozen our hearts that we no longer yearn and burn? Has the clutter and noise of our lives so weaned us away from the simple, direct, and powerful words of Jesus that we can no longer see, hear, or touch him? The living Jesus still calls us to him today. As the hymn says, "Jesus calls us o'er the tumult of our life's wild, restless sea." Let us open ourselves to hear his voice anew and recognize his presence as he breaks bread and opens the Scripture.

Conclusion—Seeking the Truth in Freedom

When we speak of the whole Jesus in all the Gospels, we need to make one clarification. It is not our goal, nor is it possible, to study every passage of each Gospel in this book. Such a task would exceed our present capabilities and would give the somewhat false impression that the whole Jesus could be understood in just one book. It would also make the book excessively long. For example, the Roman Catholic scholar John Meier has devoted more than 1500 pages to the life of Jesus, and he is not yet finished! Some of your favorite passages and stories may not even be mentioned in this book as we seek to give true treatment rather than exhaustive treatment.

As we do so, however, we are conscious of Jesus' exhortations to all of us, scholar and layperson alike, in John 8. After giving a sermon that resulted in many people believing in him, Jesus gave a gentle warning. The goal of learning about him is not merely the accumulation of knowledge; it is to continue or remain in his word. "If you continue in my word, you are truly my disciples, and you will know the truth, and the truth will make you free" (John 8:31–32). The first step is to continue in his word, to "read, mark and inwardly digest it" as the Episcopal Book of Common Prayer has it. To continue in his word is to read it, study it and live it, to have it on our lips, in our hearts, and in our steps. Only then do we become his disciples.

Discipleship doesn't happen immediately, but as a result of continuing in Jesus' words. Discipleship comes from the word "discipline" which suggests that we cannot become instant disciples. We want instant pictures, food and conveniences in our culture, but it will not be so with our discipleship. Only with the "discipline of discipleship," then, will we come to know the truth. Truth is the product of study and living, of continuing in Jesus' words, of discipleship. My hope is to be able to make clear Jesus' words and actions in this book so we all can learn how to continue in them. For if we learn that, *then* we will know the truth. We do not benefit from the truth of the Gospel until we learn to continue in the word of Jesus. Only then do we realize the beautiful promise that we shall know the truth and the truth shall make us free.

Our freedom comes as we continue in his word, as we then become disciples, as we learn the nature of the truth that is in Jesus. Freedom is the end of discipleship, not the beginning. Freedom flows from a life lived in the truth of Jesus. It is that discipleship, that truth, that freedom to which the living Jesus invites us today. Won't you join me in "learning of him"? Won't you let your mind yearn and your heart burn as you rediscover, with me, the spirituality of Jesus?

Dear Jesus, open my heart. Open my eyes that I might see you and recognize your presence. Break through the clouds of confusion. Silence the voices that attempt to drown out your voice. Lord Jesus, I desire to see you, to know you, and to experience you. I desire to be your friend and you mine. Jesus, renew my heart that I might deeply experience you. Amen.

FEEDING
THE BLAZE

PART
TWO

THE INNER LIFE
OF JESUS

THE AWAKENING OF JESUS' CALL

With the drawing of this Love and the voice of this Calling
We shall not cease from exploration And the end of all our
exploring Will be to arrive where we started And know the
place for the first time.

—T. S. Eliot, *Four Quartets*

The life of faith, the life of spirituality, is built upon God's
call of us, God's *choice* of us. Jesus said to his disciples:

You did not choose me but I chose you. And I appointed you
to go and bear fruit, fruit that will last (John 15:16).

Paul taught the same thing with different words:

Do you not know . . . that you are not your own? For you
were bought with a price; therefore glorify God in your body
(1 Cor. 6:19–20).

The call of God is the *claim* of God on us. It is God's declaration of ownership of our lives and our service.

From a human perspective, however, the call of God is a *consciousness* or awareness that, "I belong—body and soul, in life
and in death—not to myself but to my faithful Savior, Jesus
Christ, who at the cost of his own blood has fully paid for all
my sins and has completely freed me from the dominion of the
devil" (*Heidelberg Catechism*, question 1). At times the aware-

ness of our call may be vibrant, the felt presence of God very strong, and the fellowship with God's people intimate. At other times the sense of the call may be faint. Some Christians can point to a very specific moment of dramatic power where the call of God became overwhelmingly present and potent; others speak of the call of God as a gradual dawning, a heightened awareness, a spiritual nudge, a gentle bidding that only slowly took root in their lives.

Yet in every case in which a Christian sees his or her life guided by a gracious God, the call of God gives a new dimension of meaning to life. It means that our lives are not fully circumscribed by our circumstances or defined by our difficulties, that our lives are precious in God's sight and that they are directed by the God of the universe.

Many Christians segment the concept of call into several categories, such as the call to discipleship, the call to service, the call to a particular vocation, the call to a location or position, or even the call to marriage or singleness. As I read the New Testament and study the history of theology, however, I see that the principal ways to understand call are (1) the invitation to be a disciple of Jesus and 2) the pursuit of one's vocation (from the Latin *voco*—"I call") or one's life work. I derive the latter point from the leaders of the Protestant Reformation of the sixteenth century. One of their insights is the "sanctification of vocation," the belief that each task, if done to the glory of God, is as much a call of God as the call to the monastic life was to medieval Catholicism.

The Crisis of Call in Contemporary Christianity

Though the concept of call has a long history and a firm biblical grounding, it is, under the pressure of life in the late twentieth century, losing its force in our lives. There is a crisis in the *language of call*, in the *definition of the professions* and in the *lives of baby boomers and Generation X'ers*. The results are a great sense of aimlessness, increasing cases of depression, especially among middle-aged men, and a growing sense of root-lessness and loss among many Christians.

When I speak about a crisis in the *language of call,* I mean that the word is either *overused* to such an extent as to be rendered useless, or it is *avoided* at all costs. The word *call* is often an "insider's" word, a password among the supposedly spiritual elite that suggests a special relationship between the person and God. For example, I have heard people talk with great passion and certainty about how God's call has guided them through every activity of the past week. It is difficult to disagree with a person with so much certainty about God, but it makes the rest of us seem spiritually second-class, or perhaps somewhat deaf to the clear direction of the Spirit of God.

On the other hand, many Christian professional people prefer the modern language of strategic planning, goals and objectives, and are reluctant to use language of call. They are more comfortable analyzing problems and prospects in terms of the SWOC words: "Strengths, Weaknesses, Opportunities and Challenges." Even when speaking of the future of the church or possible new directions in their own lives, their decision-making model seems to be a cost-benefit analysis which leaves little room for concepts of call or the work of the Spirit.

As a result, the word *call* is either overused or unused in much Christian discourse. If we overuse the word, we run the risk of trivializing it. If we don't use it at all, we lose the impact of a central concept of faith. A balance is needed.

The second crisis affects the *professions.* Many professions have changed so dramatically in the last two decades that they are only minimally like the "calls" that many people expected. I am thinking specifically of the professions of ministry, teaching, medicine and law, though numerous other examples could be added. For example, many people understand ministry to be the process of bringing people to faith and nurturing their growth, yet it is increasingly becoming program- and management-driven. A catch phrase in ministry today is that baby boomers, whom everyone seems to want in their church, are "program-oriented people." They want formal lessons for their children, classes for their dogs and structured courses of study for themselves. Therefore, pastors must provide lots of structured opportunities for growth, which require a lot of planning. One pastor, in frustration, said to me, "How I wish I could just have *one* good talk about faith with someone, anyone, without feeling that I need to rush away immediately to plan another event."

Medicine has also changed. Doctors who entered the field with a strong desire to serve people are now feeling burdened with the reams of forms they must complete. Lawyers who entered the profession to be "counselors at law" are now leaving in droves because of the viciousness of legal practice today. Many lawyer friends have tried to dissuade me from entering law school because the profession is no longer attractive to them, and they want to do me a favor by warning me.

The crisis that results is that the professions, which were once viewed as noble vocations or "calls," are increasingly being seen simply as jobs, ways to make some money or to ensure one's future. Sometime in middle age the person asks, "Is *this* what I thought I was called to?" A person tends to question his or her call when idealism is replaced by the hard realities of the "job," and again when the profession itself undergoes such dramatic changes.

Third, there is a crisis among the *baby boomers and Generation X'ers* which affects one's call. Studies have shown, and our experience bears it out, that those born after 1945 will undergo an average of at least four career changes during their working lives. This does *not* mean they will hold four different jobs in the same field, but that second-, third- and fourth-career people will become the norm as we enter the twenty-first century. There is nothing wrong with this, even though most of us were taught that we would probably stay in one job most of our lives. However, it tends to weaken our understanding of vocation or call. Where is our call if we change careers every five years?

The result of our contemporary crisis with the idea of call is that incidents of depression, especially among middle-aged men, are increasing, as is the general feeling of aimlessness and even uselessness among many talented people. I believe there is a vast reservoir of talent in this country that isn't being developed or used. Perhaps it has been overlooked by institutions where it should have been welcomed. As one friend said to me, "I have such a clear sense of call to be a college teacher, but it seems that no administrator has received the call to recognize it!" Modern society needs to reaffirm the value of call. Its complexity and pleasure needs to be recaptured. Its pain must be recognized. Our lives depend on it.

The Call of Jesus

The call of God was central to the life of Jesus. I hope to show that by studying Jesus and his call by God, we may be encouraged to recognize and gratefully affirm our own calls. A major point will be that Jesus' awareness of the claim of God on his life grew and was clarified as he "increased in wisdom and in years, and in divine and human favor" (Luke 2:52). As we study the early chapters of the Gospels, we will focus on four ideas from Luke's Gospel: The Mystery of the Call (Luke 1:26–56), The Drama of the Call (Luke 3:21–22), The Testing of the Call (Luke 4:1–13) and, finally, The Burden of the Call (Luke 4:16–30). I will also use parallel stories in the other Gospels if they shed light on the subject I am studying.

The Mystery of the Call (Luke 1:26–56)

God's call to Jesus started before his birth. It was a mystery, even before conception occurred. It began with a willing young woman, an angel visitant and an astonishing conversation. God's call to Jesus didn't just include Jesus, as God's call in our lives doesn't begin with us. Many of us stress our uniqueness, independence and pursuit of happiness to the point that we often don't see ourselves tied into the web of life, consisting of generations of people before and after us. A living tissue of relationships connects us to people before us and around us. We are shaped by the genes and the hopes of our ancestors. Our call, in fact, begins before we are born with our parents and their forebears, whether they were people of faith or not. To find ourselves, we often need to discover how we are the children of our parents and how they were the children of their parents.

The Bible recognizes and teaches that identity is shaped before birth. Psalm 139 refers to God's knowledge of us before we were born:

> I praise you, for I am fearfully and wonderfully made.
> Wonderful are your works;
> that I know very well.
> My frame was not hidden from you,
> when I was being made in secret,
> intricately woven in the depths of the earth.
> Your eyes beheld my unformed substance (vverse
>   14–16).

The prophet Jeremiah knew that this was true of God.

> Now the word of the Lord came to me saying,
> "Before I formed you in the womb I knew you,
> and before you were born I consecrated you;
> I appointed you a prophet to the nations" (Jer. 1:4–5).

Even Job, that most persistent critic of his friends and God, confessed the same:

> Did you not pour me out like milk
> and curdle me like cheese?
> You clothed me with skin and flesh,
> and knit me together with bones and sinews (Job 10:10–11).

Some Christian denominations practice infant baptism as a sign that God has begun his work in us before we are able to respond. One mystery of the call is that it starts before we even exist. Other mysteries of Jesus' call are: (1) it started in *paradox,* (2) it was nurtured by *women;* and (3) it had *broad meaning.*

The *paradox* of Jesus' call is that it came through an unmarried woman (Luke 1:26–37). An unmarried woman would bear the Son of God. In order to receive this message, the woman was addressed by an angel. Rabbinic literature testifies to how it was improper for a young woman, under many circumstances, to speak to a man. How much more extraordinary, then, for such a woman to speak with an angel! How is it possible that such a woman, without status, was greeted by the heavenly visitor with the words, "Greetings, favored one! The Lord is with you" (Luke 1:28)? How could a woman of such low estate be favored by the Lord? Further, the Greek word translated "favored" is in the perfect tense which suggests Mary had been favored by the Lord for quite some time. So, why did the greeting to Mary seem to be so surprising and out of place to her? The paradoxes, or apparent contradictions, pile up.

So astonishing was the news that Mary would have a son that she hurried to her relative, Elizabeth, with the news (Luke 1:39–45). Together, they shared the excitement of their pregnancies and *nurtured* the call of the two boys in their wombs.

This was the first of several instances where Jesus' life was nurtured by the care of women. When he was preaching throughout Galilee and the Twelve were with him, several women were with Jesus' company who "provided for them out of their resources" (Luke 8:1–3). At the cross, when Jesus was abandoned by almost all of his disciples, he could look down and see women, nurturing him in his suffering (John 19:25–27). Finally, on the day of resurrection, women were the first to go to Jesus' tomb and were among the first witnesses of his resurrection (Luke 24; John 20).

The conversation between the pregnant women, Mary and Elizabeth, is full of gratitude, blessing and unexpected recognition of Jesus. The gratitude and blessing that fill the passage come from the instinctive feelings of Mary and Elizabeth that they were honored links in the chain of history. Their intimate conversation was nurtured by the realization that they were the bearers not just of their own lives, but of the future as well.

The call before Jesus' birth also has a *broad meaning* (Luke 1:46–56). In this passage Mary speaks the Magnificat, her hymn of praise to God for the unexpected and inexpressible pleasure of bearing the Son of God. Drawing on a rich collection of Old Testament passages, Mary speaks of the meaning of this event for herself and for others. For her it means that God has lifted her up and given her an eternal status of blessedness. For others, it means that God will also lift them up and cast down the mighty from their thrones. God is a God who brings reversal, a God who "has filled the hungry with good things, and the rich he has sent away empty" (1:53). What God has done to Mary personally will be done to others on a more universal scale.

The Drama of the Call (Luke 3:21–22)

So how did the call of God come to Jesus? How does the call of God come to us, to our conscious selves? How are we called to discipleship? How do we determine our vocation? Is call synonymous with just doing what we like to do or what we can do easily? Does call become clear to us gradually or through an experience of blinding clarity?

By examining the life of Jesus we recognize several things about call. The most important concept is that call is more an inner drive or compulsion than a preference or choice. It has a dimension of necessity to it, and it includes the anticipation of great pleasure and great pain. For Jesus it meant that he *had* to be about his Father's business (Luke 2:49) and that his destiny would be realized in Jerusalem. It was almost as if Jesus had no choice in the matter. But here is another paradox: Jesus lived in true freedom, but was under the constraints of time and the call of God.

The prophet Jeremiah experienced frequent pain as a result of God's call and often protested to God. Jeremiah thought his call should insulate him from human schemes and from the hatred of those in powerful places. In fact, his call to be a

46

prophet alienated him from people and led to several sessions of inner torment. (See, for example, Jeremiah 20:7–18.)

Jesus' call meant pain for him and for others. The prophet Simeon warned Jesus' mother:

> This child is destined for the falling and rising of many in Israel, and to be a sign that will be opposed so that the inner thoughts of many will be revealed—and a sword will pierce your own soul too (Luke 2:34–35).

Did the call of God come to Jesus gradually or in an act of blinding clarity? Both. In the passage we will now examine (Luke 3:21–22), it came with power and heavenly assurance. But as we will see it only started Jesus on the road to his life-work, and did not give him a clear blueprint for action.

> Now when all the people were baptized, and when Jesus also had been baptized and was praying, the heaven was opened, and the Holy Spirit descended upon him in bodily form like a dove. And a voice came from heaven, "You are my Son, the Beloved; with you I am well pleased."

Though many points could be made from this passage about the call of Jesus, the one that is most significant to me is that the heavenly words only *started* Jesus on the road to his full call. There is an ambiguity to these words that no doubt concerned Jesus in the wilderness. The ambiguity has to do with the meaning of the sentence.

The first half ("You are my Son, the Beloved") comes from Psalm 2:7. The second half ("With you I am well pleased") is from Isaiah 42:1. Psalm 2 talks about the coronation of the *king* of Israel, who is referred to as a Son of God. If Jesus heard the first half of the verse only, he might think that he was being called to a royal mission, perhaps a mission to bring political independence to the people of Israel. Some of Jesus' disciples believed this was his mission (Acts 1:6).

But Isaiah 42 refers to the mission of the *servant* of Yahweh: "He will not cry or lift up his voice, or make it heard in the street . . . he will faithfully bring forth justice" (verses 2–3). The servant of Yahweh will bring about the will of God through the quiet and patient work of service rather than by sovereign rule. So, which is it to be?

The calling of Jesus is laced with ambiguity. Two images not easily compatible with each other, that of servant and that of king, are placed side by side and both attributed to Jesus. How could both be true? Is the servant of Isaiah 42 the king of Psalm 2? Should Jesus be like a king the first half of his ministry and *then* like a servant? Does one of the two roles take precedence over the other? Or, in fact, are the two (servant and king) really one? How, then, are they compatible? What would that mean about how Jesus should pursue his task? How, indeed, could he be both at once? What would that look like? How much should he strive to mold himself into what he though the servant and the king should be? Or should he just try to live his life with God as his focus, and believe that somehow all things will "work out?" Should he strive to become what he was called to be?

The next forty days in the wilderness was as much a time of contemplating the call as fighting the devil, as much an attempt to interpret the will of God as to prepare himself for his life's task. Jesus' call, though accompanied with a descending dove and a heavenly voice, did not answer all his questions. As a matter of fact, it provoked more questions than it answered. It was only the beginning.

The Testing of the Call (Luke 4:1–13)

A call, to be genuine, must be tested. A sense of call might initially bring joy or satisfaction, but when it is refined it may turn out to be no more than a whim or a moment of indulged pleasure. An untested weapon creates an uncertain soldier. The Bible recognizes the importance of the testing of faith, of the testing of call. Speaking of our faith, James says:

> My brothers and sisters, whenever you face trials of any kind, consider it nothing but joy, because you know that the testing

of your faith produces endurance; and let endurance have its full effect, so that you may be mature and complete, lacking in nothing (1:2–4).

Peter speaks similarly:

In this [our hope] you rejoice, even if now for a little while you have had to suffer various trials, so that the genuineness of your faith—being more precious than gold that, though perishable, is tested by fire—may be found to result in praise and glory and honor when Jesus Christ is revealed (1 Peter 1:6–7).

A mark of a true call is that it *endures* in our lives. We may try to avoid it or ignore it, but it keeps gnawing at us, refusing to let go. A call is a sense of what we ought to be doing, where we belong, and how we "fit" into the varied tapestry of life. Peace with oneself and others largely rests with the ability to identify and embrace one's call. But a word of caution is in order. A call ought not always be easily identified with a particular profession or institutional affiliation. It may be much broader, such as a call to be a lover of humanity, a hospitable person, an interpreter of the word, an affirmer of beauty. These, indeed, might constitute a true identity, a true call.

The Testing of the Call Today

Perhaps none of us will ever have as dramatic a test of call as Jesus did. For forty days he was tested, "tempted by the devil," a thought I will come back to. Yet we also have ways that our call is tested. Four tests are *time, people, institutional framework,* and *diversity of the world.* Each of these may be a temptation, a test, a snare to keep us from committing to our call and the Lord of the call.

The testing of *time* relates to the expectation of how quickly and dramatically we should see results from our work. If call is genuine, we believe there should be something to show for it. But when? How long do you give it? A valid call might require years of work in obscurity without substantial recognition.

That is hard to do in our culture, which emphasizes having sufficient resources for oneself and one's family. As a matter of fact, recognition that comes too soon or too easily may actually be harmful. It might confuse us by making us think our efforts are for the applause and recognition, and not for the sake of the call. We will see how this was a concern for Jesus in the last section of this chapter.

The testing of *people* relates to the obstacles others present along the way—tasks we must perform, unreasonable demands or impossible personalities. Other people can be the biggest helps or worst hindrances to the unfolding of our call. Calls often develop in contexts that are all too political. We would love to avoid political correctness and "just do our work," but it is not always possible. Sometimes we fear that people will actually harm us and destroy our call as well.

A third way that call is tested today is through *institutional frameworks*. We often confuse call with the institutions in which we think call *must* be exercised. For example, many people who feel called to teach automatically think such a call *must mean* that they ought to teach in an established American school. Many who have spiritual gifts and a call to ministry think those things *must mean* that their call is to the ordained ministry in a Christian denomination. If an alternative opportunity arises, they think there is something wrong, that God is not hearing their prayer, and that they are being forsaken by Him. But why confuse our call with the institutions in which the call is *sometimes* worked out? Call, and not institutional location, is the bedrock of our spirituality, our life of faith.

Fourth, call is tested by the *diversity of the world*. Never before in human history have people been more able to experience such diversity. We know that Muslims and Buddhists are as devoted to their faith as we Christians are to ours. We know others who have no faith commitment. In some instances, those of other faiths or no faith at all actually act more mercifully, in a more timely fashion and more consistently than Christians do. So, in the final test of call we must ask ourselves,

"If people of diverse cultures and perspectives can be equally helpful to those in need, what is so sacred about a *Christian* commitment? Why not just try to devise a common *human language* of compassion? Why refer to call or use the explicit language of Christian faith when it will not be understood by most of the world?"

A quick example will illustrate the point. In 1993, I was an honored guest of the Saudi Arabian government and the Saudi Chambers of Commerce. I visited the country for two weeks, and was widely interviewed and photographed. In one of the interviews, I was asked to comment on some of the differences between the Saudi Kingdom and the United States. Never one to decline such an invitation, I began by discussing the different roles that religion played in each culture. Though the journalists had been deferential and accommodating, as soon as I brought up Christian faith and its importance for me and our culture, a distinct chill replaced the prior warmth.

All of these are modern temptations to treat call as something less than it is. These tests are real and must be addressed if we are to be faithful to God, the Lord of the call.

The Testing of Jesus' Call

I have already said that there was an ambiguity to Jesus' initial call. How did his tasks of servant and king relate? Jesus would need to mull over the problem, coax meaning from the dilemma, and then choose a life path that best exemplified his call. He needed some time to think the matter over. The Scriptures mention that Jesus was "led by the Spirit for forty days in the wilderness, to be tempted by the devil" (Luke 4:1–2). Jesus was led by God into his time of testing.

The wilderness is a place where the loyalty of the people of God is tested. It is a special place of quiet where God renews his love for his people. For forty years after the Exodus from Egypt, God led the Israelites through a forbidding wilderness. It was a time of miraculous provision by God and unfounded complaints by the people. Yet their wilderness wanderings were primarily a time of testing where they learned the habit of daily trust in the God of the Exodus.

The testing of Jesus' call came most dramatically through the temptations of the devil. I will mention only one of them here, the one that in many ways must have been the most alluring. I will try to show how the temptation to take authority over all the kingdoms of the world must have shaken Jesus to his very core.

> Then the devil led him up and showed him in an instant all the kingdoms of the world. And the devil said to him, "To you I will give their glory and all this authority; for it has been given over to me, and I give it to anyone I please. If you, then will worship me, it will all be yours" (Luke 4:5–7).

A few questions arise immediately. How did these words come to Jesus? Were they audibly spoken? Felt only deep in the recesses of his consciousness? More importantly, did Jesus *know* the words were those of the devil? The Gospel writers had no doubt of it, but as I reflect on the nature of temptation and the biblical presentation of Satan, perhaps Jesus wasn't sure who was speaking to him. Satan's greatest weapon is his ability to deceive. After forty years of hindsight, Luke and Matthew could write forthrightly that the temptation was from the devil. If that had been as clear to Jesus, it would take away some of the power of the temptation.

A good illustration can be found in *Pilgrim's Progress,* the great seventeenth Century Puritan classic and allegory of the Christian life. It begins with the call of Christian (the main character) from the City of Destruction and ends with his entrance into the Heavenly City. Along the way he meets many trials and temptations. The most fearful trial takes place in the Valley of the Shadow of Death, where Christian meets Apollyon, the foe from hell. At first their fight is with weapons. Christian manages to beat his opponent because he has outfitted himself with "the whole armor of God." But then there is a more frightening encounter. The Evil One begins to give Christian thoughts of unfaithfulness and desertion, and Christian becomes very confused because he cannot identify the different voices in his mind. Which is the voice of God? Which is the voice of Satan? Which is the voice of his own troubled mind? Deception, indeed, creates a terrible form of trial and temptation.

The temptation of Jesus was a real, serious and possibly fatal deception. But the deception was not simply a result of *who* was speaking to Jesus; it also related to *what was said*. The second temptation concerned the authority over all the kingdoms of the world. Let us examine why this was a subtle, yet powerful temptation.

God's Word after Jesus' baptism, "You are my Son, the Beloved," was a reference to Psalm 2:7, indicating that Jesus, in some way, was the kingly Son of God. The next verse in Psalm 2 reads as follows:

> Ask of me, and I will make the nations your heritage,
> and the ends of the earth your possession (Ps. 2:8).

After God's acknowledgment of Jesus' sonship, the Son is entitled to ask for authority over the nations. Certainly while Jesus was in the wilderness, he had this passage in his mind. He had been identified as the Son. He knew that after being declared Son, he is authorized to ask of God and God would make the nations his heritage. If he were to follow the Scriptures, he could ask and be given the nations as his heritage. This was precisely the devil's second temptation: "To you I will give their glory and all this authority" (Luke 4:6). The words that came to Jesus in the wilderness arise from the thought of Psalm 2:8, the verse *after* the declaration of sonship. Wouldn't Jesus have thought that the words he heard *must* have been the Word of God? "I am the Son; I ask; I receive the nations. That is exactly what is being presented to me now! Why delay?" The voice within or the voice without was asking for his worship in exchange. Why not give it, for certainly the logic of the words was the logic of the Word of God?

In a sense, the second temptation of Jesus was to rely *too* heavily on a passage of Scripture that he had already relied upon! It may sound strange to put it this way, but unless we feel the unsettling nature of the second temptation and the profound uncertainty that it must have created in Jesus, we don't realize the power of the test. The careful reader of Scripture should, at this point, be almost as exhausted as Jesus must have been. Ultimately, Jesus decided to use another scriptural reference about worshiping God alone to solve the uncertainty created by the devil's allusion to Psalm 2:8. His knowledge of Scripture, plus a heart attuned to the rhythms of God's timing in his life, helped Jesus survive.

The Burden of the Call (Luke 4:16–30)

The burden of the call of God includes the weight we feel, the compulsion that drives us and the need we have to express the call and to live it fully. Our call, Jesus' call, must not only be received and tested; it must also be expressed regularly through the actions of our lives. But just as the word *burden* can suggest something that is either light or heavy, so our call can have elements of lightness and heaviness to it.

The call of false gods can create quite a burden, such as the weighty idols of the Babylonians, Bel and Nebo, after the destruction of Babylon:

Bel bows down, Nebo stoops,
their idols are on beasts and cattle;
these things you carry are loaded as burdens on weary
    animals.
They stoop, they bow down together (Isa. 46:1–2).

In contrast, the call of Jesus has a lightness and ease to it. The last chorus of Part I of Handel's *Messiah* is entitled, "His Yoke Is Easy." Taken from Jesus' words in Matthew 11:28, the chorus proceeds with boundless energy. After only three quick eighth notes as an introduction, the sopranos enter with a rapid flow of sixteenth notes and even an occasional thirty-second note. The words of King James English are repeated several

THE AWAKENING OF JESUS' CALL

times, "His yoke is easy, His burthen is light." Then the tenors enter, and the altos and finally the baritones, all with a lightness and rapidity that matches the lightness of the verse from Matthew. At the end, all four parts sing in a rich harmony, concluding with a slow fortissimo, "and his burthen is light." The music loudly proclaims the lightness of the call of God.

The call of Jesus will include both light and heavy experiences. Both, indeed, are included in his first words in the Gospel of Luke (4:16–30). Within the scope of fifteen verses Jesus goes from *favorite son* to *despised enemy* of the people. Though we could examine this passage from many angles, we want to consider it briefly from the perspective of the burden of the call. The fundamental point we will make is that the burden of the call of God requires us to tell the truth, even when the consequences may be adverse to us.

The situation is memorable. The local boy, Jesus, returns home, joins the community in worship and stands to read and interpret the Scripture. He selects a passage from Isaiah 61:1–2 and alters it slightly:

> The Spirit of the Lord is upon me,
> because he has anointed me
> to bring good news to the poor.
> He has sent me to proclaim release to the captives
> and recovery of sight to the blind,
> to let the oppressed go free,
> to proclaim the year of the Lord's favor (Luke 4:18–19).

It is a wonderful selection. Both liberals and conservatives would appreciate the passage. It talks about spiritual liberation, but one can also hear a political message in the passage. Those who hated the Roman occupation could find solace in the text. Those who only wanted a message of spiritual comfort could benefit from its cadences. Thus, it is not surprising that the popular response to Jesus' reading was that "all spoke well of him" (verse 22). Local boy returns home and dazzles the congregation. How wonderful.

The situation was calculated to enhance the feeling of good will between the people and Jesus. It was a religious context, a sort of reunion for Jesus, and he read a popular passage from a popular prophet. What speaker could have hoped for a better response to his or her first words? Yet as Jesus continued to speak, the situation changed drastically. He had them in the palm of his hand, but soon they were at his throat.

> They got up, drove him out of the town, and led him to the brow of the hill on which their town was built, so that they might hurl him off the cliff (verse 29).

Why did the people become upset with Jesus? Why didn't Jesus stop speaking when he still had their support? The people were upset with Jesus because he told them the Scriptures would be fulfilled but the congregation at Nazareth would not be recipients of this fulfillment.

> Truly I tell you, no prophet is accepted in the prophet's hometown. But the truth is, there were many widows in Israel in the time of Elijah, when the heaven was shut up three years and six months, and there was a severe famine over all the land; yet Elijah was sent to none of them except to a widow at Zarephath in Sidon. There were also many lepers in Israel in the time of the prophet Elisha, and none of them was cleansed except Naaman the Syrian (Luke 4:24–27).

In ancient days, Elijah and Elisha had performed great works to people outside of Israel. So it would be with Jesus. He was *from* Nazareth, but he wasn't sent *to* them. And to make matters a bit worse, Jesus called their faith into question. His words were direct and even offensive. The anger of the congregation was understandable.

But why would Jesus have said such a thing to inaugurate his ministry? Why pick a fight when he didn't have to? And how was this related to his call? Didn't Jesus make a colossal miscalculation? I think that Jesus responded to their adulation in the way he did because he realized, in the core of his being, that popularity was dangerous, fickle, and even false. He knew instinctively that if people *really knew* him and his ministry, most would have nothing to do with him. He wasn't simply an entertainer, sent to heal a few people and impress the rest. The burden of his call required acting in a way that would lead him into conflict with people. He had to fulfill his emerging understanding of himself as servant and king. If he responded to the popular acclaim with deference, if he fed on their adulation, he would become captive to it. A popular person has to keep being popular through an endless cycle of performances, each of which must equal or surpass the last.

Jesus decided, at the outset of his ministry, to be faithful to the burden of the call rather than seek the acclaim of the people. His subsequent ministry proved what he already knew—that when the going got tough, he would be abandoned by many of his early well-wishers. The burden of Jesus' call meant that he had to reject popularity, even among religious people. What is emerging for us is a picture of Jesus which we will continue to develop. He was a man of substance, of grit, of serious and even severe purpose, of extreme self-awareness from the beginning of his ministry. He was so because he knew the dynamics of the call of God. He heard its inner rhythm and oriented his life to its insistent bidding. No other voice, no matter how alluring, affirming or seemingly authoritative, would be able to coax him away from that steady, sweet, burdensome call of God.

Jesus, awaken within me a call, a passion. Kindle within me a fire, a blaze. Burn within my heart. Let your truth burn within my soul. Dear Jesus, awaken within me a call, a passion to be more like you, to understand and to grow in the knowledge of your love. So many times this passion is missing. I simply want to satisfy my own pleasures. I want to follow the patterns and the passions of this world. But Lord Jesus, I know that you understand this, for you were tempted as I am tempted, and yet you did not sin. Jesus, I deeply desire this burning spirit within me, of burning love, of burning grace, of burning truth. May it ignite every aspect of my soul and deeply move me into a deeper communion with you. Awaken within me this call Lord Jesus, this passion, this desire, this fire. Amen.

3

JESUS AND THE MASTERY OF SCRIPTURE

> In order to arrive at what you do not know You must go by a
> way which is the way of ignorance. . . . And what you do not
> know is the only thing you know . . .
>
> —T. S. Eliot, *Four Quartets*

From the beginning to the end of Jesus' ministry, Scripture was on his lips. When the devil challenged him to turn stones into bread, Jesus replied in the words of the Old Testament, "One does not live by bread alone" (Luke 4:4, quoting Deut. 8:3). On the day of his resurrection, just before he left his disciples, "he opened their minds to understand the scriptures" (Luke 24:45). Jesus found his life in the Scriptures. They not only provided guidance and strength for daily living, but also gave him a pattern for living and a structure in which to understand his entire ministry. The Scriptures governed his life, imparted values, guided his action. He found God there, and he found himself also.

Jesus mastered the scriptures. It is not unusual for devout people of the Middle East to memorize their sacred text, word for word. But even those who have learned their sacred text, whether it is the Bible or the Koran, know that memorizing is only the *first* step in mastery. Beyond memorization is meditation, singing the text, and incorporating insights from it into one's life, one's vocabulary and even the very marrow of one's being. The rhythms of the text become the rhythms of one's own life. The Scriptures become a living stream. They feed the soul and form the life.

The process of mastery is a rewarding one and is guided by a few simple principles. First, mastery is *driven by desire*. Mastery starts with the heart. As heart and mind work in conjunction, insights develop and skills are refined. Mastery requires the learning of methods and skills, and empathy with others who have also tried to master the text. In a moving passage in an early canto of Dante's *Inferno*, Dante is invited by some of the great bards of the past, such as Homer and Virgil, to join their company. Thus, before Dante can demonstrate the skills of his own mastery, he must become a member of the great group of poets of Western culture.

Second, in order to master something, you must *first be mastered by it*. In order to become a master, you must submit yourself to a master. The master, whether it is a person or a text or a skill, needs to probe you, correct you, enlighten you, and test you in order to see if you are up to the task of mastery. Mastery is not something casually offered or easily attained; the society of masters is elite indeed. You have to submit yourself to the text in order to hear the lessons of the master. Sometimes the lessons will be obvious. Other times they are communicated subtly, so that only those with ears to hear and eyes to see will understand them. Mastery has its own lessons to teach and its own rhythms to hear. It will yield rewards, but they will be won only after great struggle. We may try to impose ourselves on the text or to wrest victory from the master, but such Pyrrhic victories come only at the cost of losing ourselves in the process.

Third, the process of mastery is a *process of slow building*. As astonishing insights become evident, they are meant to provide incentive and encouragement—something like getting a second wind or discovering an unexpected dramatic vista on a mountain climb. The Scriptures or the skill only slowly adhere to our memories. We often forget more than we learn. But eventually it becomes united to us, merged with us, and we know we are on the way to mastery.

Loving God, Loving Scripture

The people of Israel were aware of the value of mastery of the Scriptures. A good Jew would recite the Shema (a prayer affirming faith in God) daily. It reads,

> Hear O Israel: The Lord is our God, the Lord alone. You shall love the Lord your God with all your heart, and with all your soul, and with all your might. Keep these words that I am commanding you today in your heart. Recite them to your children and talk about them when you are at home and when you are away, when you lie down and when you rise. Bind them as a sign on your hand, fix them as an emblem on your forehead, and write them on the doorposts of your house and on your gates (Deut. 6:4–9).

Love of God and mastery of Scripture go hand in hand. Loving God with all one's heart means that God's Word is constantly on one's heart. What is the expected result if love of God and mastery of Scripture become priorities? Success in one's endeavors. Note, the Lord's instructions to Joshua:

> This book of the law shall not depart out of your mouth; you shall meditate on it day and night, so that you may be careful to act in accordance with all that is written in it. For then you shall make your way prosperous, and then you shall be successful (Josh. 1:8).

Psalms 1, 19 and 119 are a triad of writings which celebrate the value of the mastery and love of Scripture. Psalm 119 is the Psalm of Scripture mastery and the glory of the Law of God *par excellence*. It consists of eight-verse stanzas, each beginning with a successive letter of the Hebrew alphabet (which has 22 letters). By beginning each stanza with the next letter of the Hebrew alphabet, the author demonstrates that the Scripture addresses life from the beginning to the end or, as we would say, from A to Z.

Four characteristics of Scripture brought to light from Psalm 119 are its *sweetness*, its *value*, its role in *bringing understanding* and its *sheer delight*. "How sweet are your words to my taste, sweeter than honey to my mouth!" (verse 103) The prophet Ezekiel also discovered the sweetness of the Word of God when God commanded him to take and eat a scroll. "Then I ate it; and in my mouth it was as sweet as honey" (Ezekiel 3:3).

If the Lord gives us a sweet Word, the very Word of God, what are we to do? "O taste and see that the Lord is good" (Ps. 34:8). Blessed are those who know the sweet taste of the Scripture. Are our taste buds attuned to it?

The Scripture is not only sweet; it is of *great value*. A recurring theme in Psalms 19 and 119 is that the Word of God is more valuable than gold. "The law of your mouth is better to me than thousands of gold and silver pieces" (Ps. 119:72; see also verse 127 and 19:10). If our values are steeped in biblical values, we will value Scripture more than any other treasure.

What is the result of treasuring the Scripture, of enjoying its taste? It brings great *joy and understanding*. Proper understanding of the Scriptures gives a person more insight than teachers or experienced older people (Ps. 119:99–100). "Through your precepts I get understanding; therefore I hate every false way" (Ps. 119:104). "Your decrees are my delight, they are my counselors" (verse 24).

These are a few of the scriptural promises that must have seeped deeply into Jesus' mind and shaped his character. They taught him that the mastery of the Scriptures was key to laying a firm foundation in life. Like the householder who dug deeply and built his house on the firm foundation of Jesus' words (Luke 6:46–48), Jesus himself dug deeply and founded his house on the Word of God. He taught others to do so, because he had already learned the benefit of deep digging and careful building.

We will follow Jesus through the Gospels and study the way the Scriptures functioned for him in everyday life. Though we can only scratch the surface of the topic, we will examine it under four headings: (1) The life-giving Word; (2) The ethics of scriptural mastery; (3) Internalizing the Scripture; and (4) Scripture explodes.

The Life-giving Word

Jesus' first use of Scripture that we are told about came when he was tempted by the devil (Luke 4:1–13). He had spent forty days without food in the wilderness, mulling over the call of God, trying to understand the meaning of the heavenly words at his baptism. In Jesus' time of physical need, the devil came to him and encouraged him to use his powers as the Son of God to transform stones into bread. Instead of acceding to his request, Jesus responded, "It is written, 'One does not live by bread alone'" (Luke 4:4).

In Jesus' response we not only see his knowledge of Scripture, but also the way his mind worked in applying Scripture. In this case, and in the next temptation also, Jesus' mind worked like a *concordance* of Scripture, while in the third temptation his mind acted like a *thesaurus*. A concordance lists all the appearances of a word in Scripture. A thesaurus is a book of synonyms which opens up a larger conceptual field to the word than a dictionary would. A thesaurus is, literally, a "treasury" of words that, as it were, mines every vein in a rock formation for similarities with the word under consideration. A concordance looks for exact word matches while a thesaurus tries to suggest relationships between words or concepts that may not have occurred to the person who used the word.

When we see how Jesus used Scripture during his temptations, we see a brilliant mind which knew how to read Scripture literally as well as imaginatively. The devil urged him to change stones to bread. It was an attempt to convince Jesus to supply his own need in his hungry state. Jesus knew his need and what bread could do to fulfill it, but he was also aware of Scripture teaching that bread was not the basic sustaining principle of life. He applied a scriptural passage that used the word "bread," but used it in a way that would glorify God rather than satisfying his own physical appetite.

A similar thing happened in the second temptation. The devil offered Jesus authority over all earthly kingdoms if Jesus would bow down and worship him. Despite the power of this temptation, Jesus again focused on a particular word, this time *worship,* and found a reference in the Scriptures that fit his need: "Worship the Lord your God, and serve only him" (Luke 4:8, quoting Deut. 6:13). Jesus' *concordance-like* knowledge of Scriptures allowed him to clarify the same words used by the devil. This kind of Scriptural mastery helped him through the first two temptations.

But it should be noted that when a person has a concordance-like mind, the crucial issue becomes *how* to choose one text over another when both use the desired word. For example, why did Jesus choose Deuteronomy 8:3 ("One does not live by bread alone") rather than Exodus 16:4 ("I am going to rain bread from heaven for you")? In fact, Jesus might have cited the latter verse as a justification for why he *should* turn the stones into bread. But he didn't. Why not? It is here that one goes not only to the mind of Jesus but to his heart also.

The mastery of Scripture is, in fact, a discipline of the heart. In Jesus' heart, the most important principle was to bring honor to God. Anything that detracted from the honor of God was, by its very nature, undesirable. The transformation of rocks into bread or the premature control over all the kingdoms of the world carried with them the danger that the Son would be exalted over the Father, and that the honor of the Father might thereby be reduced. So Jesus complemented his concordance-like mind with a deeper spiritual principle: *preservation of the honor of God.* Consequently, the temptations were turned aside. Scripture surely gave life to Jesus' answers, but it was Scripture applied toward preserving the honor of God.

The third temptation shows Jesus' use of Scripture in a slightly different fashion. In this case, the devil himself uses Scripture to encourage Jesus to make a great display of himself by leaping down from the pinnacle of the temple in Jerusalem. Many people would see this action and become immediate followers of Jesus. To support his case, the devil quoted a passage from the Psalms to the effect that God's angels would bear Jesus up so he wouldn't even strike his foot against a stone (Ps. 91:11–12).

In this instance, Jesus gave a *thesaurus-like* rather than a *concordance-like* answer to the devil. He didn't recite Scripture passages with the word "hand" or "angel" in them, though there were certainly many he could have used. Rather, he looked at the whole nature of what was being proposed, and sought a "synonym" for it. What the devil was proposing was for Jesus to presume on the graciousness of God or, in a word, to *tempt* God into saving him. It would be like backing God into a corner. If *you,* God, don't save me, there goes the Son of God and so much for *your* plan of salvation! The devil was really asking Jesus to presume a superiority to God by compelling God to save him. To act in this way would be tempting God. So Jesus responded, "It is said, 'Do not put the Lord your God to the test'" (Luke 4:12, quoting Deut. 6:16). So alive was the Scripture for Jesus, and so full of life-giving power, that it was his weapon of choice in dealing with the devil. Jesus' *concordance-like* and *thesaurus-like* use of Scripture in a moment of dire need proved the value of the mastery of Scripture for Jesus.

The Ethics of Scripture Mastery

When we think of Scripture mastery, we usually think in terms of an intellectual accomplishment. We think of success at Bible trivia games, ease at recalling passages, skill at identifying key biblical concepts. For Jesus, however, the mastery of Scripture had an ethical dimension. This is no more evident than in the parable of the Good Samaritan (Luke 10:25–37). It will be useful to quote the entire parable, beginning with verses 25–28.

> Just then a lawyer stood up to test Jesus. "Teacher," he said, "what must I do to inherit eternal life?" He said to him, "What is written in the law? What do you read there?" He answered,

"You shall love the Lord your God with all your heart, and with all your soul, and with all your strength, and with all your mind; and your neighbor as yourself." And he said to him, "You have given the right answer; do this, and you will live."

The question of eternal life drives the conversation. It is a most important question, and Jesus, as a skillful teacher, turned the question back on the questioner with a question of his own. It is reminiscent of the old Jewish joke where a person complains to a rabbi, "I object to your answering every question I ask with a question." To which the rabbi replies, "What is wrong with a question?"

"What is written in the law?" Jesus asks. The lawyer's response shows him to be a lover of Scripture. He combines two texts, from Deuteronomy 6:5 and Leviticus 19:18, when he responds. Nowhere in the vast literature of Judaism did anyone combine those two texts before the lawyer did in this passage. His reading of the Scripture is creative, practical and to the point.

The lawyer's reading of the Scripture also leaves one question unanswered. Who is the neighbor? Eternal life depends on loving God and one's neighbor, and Scripture and tradition are pretty explicit on the nature of the love of God. So we must press ahead and determine who the neighbor is. Fellow Jews? If so, are resident aliens included? Samaritans? Outsiders? This is a question that both the lawyer and Jesus had thought about, but Jesus' answer in the form of a parable shows that his reading, his "mastery" of the Scripture, was much more profound.

Jesus replied, "A man was going down from Jerusalem to Jericho, and fell into the hands of robbers, who stripped him, beat him, and went away, leaving him half dead. Now by chance a priest was going down that road; and when he saw him, he passed by on the other side. So likewise a Levite, when he came to the place and saw him, passed by on the other side. But a Samaritan while traveling came near him; and when he saw him, he was moved with pity. He went to him and bandaged his wounds, having poured oil and wine on them. Then he put him on his own animal, brought him to an inn, and took care of him. The next day he took out two denarii, gave them to the innkeeper, and said, 'Take care of him; and when I come back, I will repay you whatever more you spend.' Which of these three, do you think, was a neighbor to the man who fell into the hands of the robbers?' He said, 'The one who showed him mercy.' Jesus said to him, 'Go and do likewise'" (Luke 10:30–37).

A beautiful story like this only arises out of long and detailed reflection on the question that the lawyer posed. It must have been a question that Jesus had asked himself time after time. But in his hours of reflection on this question, the question changed a bit in his mind. This change is the key to understanding the ethics of Scripture mastery.

The question changed from "Who is my neighbor?" to "What does it mean to act like a neighbor?" The first question is a good one, and it seems to come right out of the biblical text. The command is to love your neighbor as yourself. The inquisitive student naturally wants to clarify the meaning of *neighbor*. But posing the question in this way turns a personal issue into an academic issue. It turns people into things or, in Martin Buber's terminology, changes a "thou" into an "it." The commandment is to *love* the neighbor, not to *identify* the neighbor.

One might plausibly argue that one must *identify* the neighbor as a necessary prerequisite for *loving* him, but Jesus was wise enough to know that the process of definition itself often leads to endless discussions and few resolutions. Various schools of thought emerge on the different ways to define a term, and one can easily become either immobilized by the various alternatives or so titillated by them as to develop one's own definition. Life then becomes the process of criticizing and suggesting definitions, rather than loving the neighbor.

By telling the story of the Good Samaritan, Jesus shows that we are not to *define* "neighbor," but to *be* a neighbor. He breaks down the ethical barrier that academic discussion might erect between the text and the heart. How does one be a neighbor? By acting mercifully. The heart of Jesus' faith is merciful action.

The heart of ethical mastery of the Scripture is to allow Scripture to move us to act mercifully. If reading Scripture doesn't lead to compassionate action, we have not read Scripture correctly. We have read it academically, legalistically. Scripture properly mastered breaks down barriers of race and ethnicity. The lawyer was a perfect foil for Jesus, though he was not criticized or belittled in the process. Actually, I believe despite so many harsh words against the teachers of the law, Jesus actually appreciated them. He knew they were the ones who wanted to keep digging deeper into the meaning of a Scripture. Their rather wooden questions, however, stimulated him to develop a whole range of more challenging questions about the Scriptures. Partially because of the lawyers, Jesus was forced to develop and refine his own philosophy of life. And the central principle of that philosophy is that life is about the heart and not simply about defining terms. Life ought to be lived at "soul intimacy" and not at arm's length. Mastery of Scripture means to live with compassion. It is as simple and as difficult as that.

Internalizing Scripture

The most important and elusive task in scriptural mastery is internalizing the Scripture. Internalizing is the step beyond reading, studying, memorizing and meditating. It is when the Scripture becomes so deeply embedded in our lives that it need not be "drawn out" and "thought about" to have an influence. It becomes part of our very soul. It shapes us and conforms to us. Its very contours become the contours of our thoughts, words and hopes. This is beyond the stage where Scripture is used to extract comforting verses or even "principles of living." To internalize the Scripture means that it becomes so much a part of us that the text begins to "play" with us and we with the text. At unpredictable times of the day or night, during serious or relaxing activity, the text returns to challenge, entertain, and present itself anew to us. Scripture becomes our most engaging conversation partner.

One of the first books written in English in the New World of the seventeenth century was the *History of Plymouth Plantations* by Governor William Bradford. That simple, straightforward narrative of the first decades of the Pilgrim community in Plymouth, Massachusetts, is so suffused with biblical phrases and cadences that Bradford's story is almost a "second Deuteronomy." The works of many other Puritan writers of that period show the same mastery of scriptural language.

More interesting for my purposes is the way that a "sacred text" played a role in the literary imagination of a contemporary American writer. Norman Maclean taught literature and poetry for years at the University of Chicago, and only started writing seriously for publication after his retirement. His most famous work, *A River Runs Through It*, was made into a major film in 1991. Yet perhaps his most riveting work is the posthumously published *Young Men and Fire*. This book is the story of the deaths of thirteen young firefighters in Mann Gulch, Montana, while battling a terrible forest fire in the summer of 1949. Maclean tells the story in excruciating detail with an elegance, tension, clarity and passion that nourish the heart.

The thing that pushes Maclean to get to the bottom of the tragedy is the question of purpose. Was there any possible purpose or good that could come from this tragedy, or must it remain forever an inexplicable catastrophe, an absurd reminder of our smallness and limited capacity as humans? Why is Maclean so persistent in asking the question of purpose? He explained that when he was a boy, his father taught him the Shorter Catechism, and the first question of that Catechism was forever emblazed on his heart. The question is, "What is the chief end of man?" The answer: "Man's chief end is to glorify God and to enjoy him forever." Maclean says that he not only memorized the question and answer, but he also absorbed the entire mode of thought *behind* the question. The first question assumes that there *is* a purpose to the universe, that humans *have* a place in it, and that God's glory *will be* the goal of faithful human striving.

Maclean continued to search for the purpose of the tragedy or, in his words, the "lessons" of it, because of an abiding conviction that there is a larger purpose to life. How did he know? Because the very rhythms of the Shorter Catechism teach it. Maclean caught its rhythms and internalized its spirit, and a great and moving work of literature was the result.

This is the kind of internalization I am referring to, where the Bible's phrases, rhythms and deep structures become so much a part of us that it even shapes the way we ask questions. This is the kind of knowledge Jesus had, and it was never so evident as in the controversy between Jesus and the Sadducees about the resurrection of the dead.

The account occurs in Matthew 22:23–33, Mark 12:18–27 and Luke 20:27–40, but our focus will be on the story as told by Mark. It appears in the midst of controversy. Jesus has told the Parable of the Wicked Tenants, and then the Jews tried to bait Jesus on the issue of paying taxes to Caesar. In that context, the Sadducees approached him and posed a problem:

> Some Sadducees, who say there is no resurrection, came to him and asked him a question, saying, "Teacher, Moses wrote for us that 'if a man's brother dies, leaving a wife but no child, the man shall marry the widow and raise up children for his brother.' There were seven brothers; the first married and, when he died, left no children; and the second married her and died, leaving no children; and the third likewise; none of the seven left children. Last of all the woman herself died. In the resurrection whose wife will she be? For the seven had married her" (Mark 12:18–23).

We don't know a lot about the Sadducees, but we do know that they only accepted the authority of the Pentateuch, the first five books of our Bible. Since the Pentateuch did not speak explicitly about the resurrection of the dead or the future life, the Sadducees did not believe in it. All other groups of Jews in Jesus' time believed in the resurrection, since later passages of the Old Testament and intertestamental writings teach it.

So the Sadducees presented a case for Jesus to solve. They did it in a such a way as to ridicule the belief in resurrection. The mere telling of the story and posing of the question is meant to discredit the belief in resurrection. They took the example of a practice commanded by Moses, known as levirate marriage (Deut. 25:5–10), in which a man was required to marry the wife of a deceased older brother if his brother's marriage had yielded no children. The purpose of the law was to assure that family land would not be lost to another family. So the Sadducees had Jesus suppose that a series of seven brothers each tried, unsuccessfully, to have a child with the same woman after each previous brother had died. Since Jesus believed in the resurrection and they didn't, they were leaving it to him to decide, whose wife she would be?

The Sadducees could count on the crowd enjoying the story and imagining the rather comical scenario of seven successive brothers dying at the hands of one wife. You can almost hear them: "What did she feed them? What did she do to them in the bedroom? I'd rather be the woman's dog than her husband!" Imagine the laughter. "Don't you see," the Sadducees seem to be saying, "that even the *thought* of the resurrection is ridiculous?"

The belief in resurrection presents problems that are insolvable. All seven brothers had an equal "share" in the woman. How could only one be "married" to her in the life to come? Or is life after resurrection just one big polygamous orgy? The Sadducees felt it was better to hold to the explicit teachings of Moses than to speculate about the resurrection.

Jesus' response to them is found in Mark 12:24–27.

> Jesus said to them, "Is not this the reason you are wrong, that you know neither the scriptures nor the power of God? For when they rise from the dead, they neither marry nor are given in marriage, but are like angels in heaven. And as for the dead being raised, have you not read in the book of Moses, in the story about the bush, how God said to him, 'I am the God of Abraham, the God of Isaac, and the God of Jacob?' He is God not of the dead, but of the living; you are quite wrong.'"

Jesus' first words set the tone for the rest of the encounter. He will show the Sadducees to be deficient in theological and biblical knowledge. His answer will demonstrate that he has internalized the Scripture to such an extent that he can confute the Sadducees on their own ground.

Jesus refers to Moses' encounter with God at the burning bush (Exod. 3:1–6). During that confrontation, God identified himself as the God of Abraham, Isaac and Jacob. He was the God of the covenant with Israel. Why would God have identified himself in this way if he wanted to give comfort to Moses? If God had delivered Abraham, Isaac, and Jacob only to let them die forever, it would be like saying, "I am a God who specializes in saving people, but only for the duration of their natural lives. When they die, that's it." To believe this would question God's power.

But the power of God is evident not simply in the fact that He delivers *living* people, but also that he gives eternal life to people *who have died*. Abraham, Isaac and Jacob form a living chorus, testifying to the faithfulness and power of God to deliver them in life *and* in death.

God is a God of life and of covenant faithfulness for all generations. He doesn't save people only to let them die forever. Therefore, the reference to Abraham, Isaac, and Jacob must not be to people who died and are still dead. When God appeared to Moses hundreds of years after the patriarchs died, He appeared as the God of the living. The patriarchs still live because of the power of God. Therefore, the Scriptures—even the Pentateuch—show that there is a resurrection.

This type of understanding requires deep reading of the Scriptures. It exceeds the depth of other rabbinic attempts to "prove" the resurrection from the Pentateuch. Rabbi Gamaliel II tried to do so using Deuteronomy 11:9 ("so that you may live long in the land that the Lord swore to your ancestors to give *them*") on the ground that the ancestors who died are also beneficiaries of the promises and, therefore, must have been given new life. But Jesus' argument is so much more rooted to the central characters of Scripture, so immediate in its impact, so powerful in its application and, best of all, so unexpected! Jesus has shown that the Scripture internalized brings unexplored depths of wisdom and insight, and leads to the honor of God.

Scripture Explodes

The Scriptures are so full, so various and so deep. They are life-giving and fruitful. They are more colorful than a Dutch garden, more harmonious than a Beethoven symphony, more refreshing than a mountain spring. They engage the heart, the soul and the mind.

> How weighty to me are your thoughts, O God! How vast is the sum of them! I try to count them—they are more than the sand (Ps. 139:17–18).

The Scripture explodes with meaning, like fireworks of the soul.

A long time ago I had a friend who tried to teach me how to interpret the Scripture. He was a fine Christian and an evangelical leader, and I remember his advice to this day. I disagree with it entirely, but it has taken me twenty-five years and a lot of study to know why.

He told me on one occasion that for every passage of the Bible there is one, and only one, correct interpretation. There may be several applications of the text to different people's lives, but only one interpretation. He encouraged me to study the Bible to seek that one true interpretation. For years I believed that there was only one meaning to a passage, one "truth" to it. But now I believe, and I think my study of Jesus confirms it, that there are several levels of meaning in the Scripture. Meaning is sometimes as various and uncontrolled as the growth of jungle vegetation. I believe, in addition, that the distinction between interpretation and application is wooden and irrelevant. As we have seen in the Parable of the Good Samaritan, Jesus tried to reduce the distinction between truth (interpretation) and action (application).

In the final passage of Scripture I will examine in this chapter, Jesus turned the tables on his opponents and asked *them* a question of Scriptural interpretation. He had resolved the supposed contradiction of the Sadducees, so he proposed his own scriptural conundrum to his hearers.

> While Jesus was teaching in the temple, he said, "How can the scribes say that the Messiah is the Son of David? David himself, by the Holy Spirit, declared, 'The Lord said to my Lord, "Sit at my right hand, until I put your enemies under your feet."' David himself calls him Lord; so how can he be his son?" And the large crowd was listening to him with delight (Mark 12:35–37).

The popular and scholarly understanding of the Messiah in the first century A.D. was that he was the Son of David. The belief was rooted in 2 Samuel 7:11–16, where Nathan prophesied to David that his throne would never lack a son to occupy it. The belief was reinforced in the Psalms and Prophets, and soon became the common designation for the messianic deliverer of the Jewish people. They awaited a "king like David," a son of David, to overthrow the Romans and establish an independent kingdom, as David had cleared Jerusalem of the Jebusites and set up the united monarchy 1,000 years previously.

But Jesus challenged this thinking by quoting the opening words of Psalm 110 in which David says, "The Lord says to my Lord, 'Sit at my right hand.'" The passage refers to two "Lords." The first one is the Lord God, but who is the other? Most Jews believed that the second "Lord" in this passage referred to the Messiah. The early Christians often applied this passage to Jesus. (See, for example, Hebrews 1:13.) Christians and Jews shared the sense that the passage had messianic overtones.

Now we are ready for the reasoning of Jesus, and a question which shows the explosive character of the Scripture. Jesus says, in effect, "If David calls him Lord, he must have already existed at the time of David. Yet the Messiah is a Son of David, to be born from his descendants. How can he already exist if he is yet to be born? How can he both be Lord and Son?"

What a question! To see that the Messiah can be both Lord and Son causes the Scripture to explode with meaning. It bursts our preconceptions of how God must act! If the scribes or Jesus wanted to "solve" this conundrum, they possibly could have done it by differentiating between physical descent and spiritual authority, but the explanation might appear to be a bit strained and abstract. Besides, Jesus used this example to demonstrate their limited way of thinking.

Jesus' problem with the scribes, both ancient *and* modern, is that they try to limit God by giving consistent and simple explanations of how he must act and how all Scriptures must be understood. Those who want only *one* interpretation for each passage are always confident they have discovered that one interpretation! Scribes, ancient and modern, are often "control-oriented" people who want to reduce faith, the Scriptures and ultimately, God, to a simple and explicable package. They justify this by saying people's faith is too fragile to live with "evasive" or "uncertain" answers. They say faith needs to be black and white, without a shade of grey! They insist people need clarity, truth, and simplicity! And, of course, the scribes offer people what they think the people need.

Jesus was not a scribe. He was their opponent. He presented the previous scriptural difficulty without clarification because he believed both statements were true, but he didn't need to explain *how* they were true. Maybe the two couldn't be reconciled easily. We often affirm two apparently contradictory statements without being able to explain them. For example, how can Christ be fully divine and fully human? How can God be present everywhere but be absent from the hearts of those who don't know him?

The fact that two scriptural statements cannot easily be reconciled is no reason to embark on complex schemes to try to reconcile all texts to our intellectual satisfaction. We need to realize that God cannot be confined to our chain of reasoning. God is bigger than our minds, than our ability to reconcile statements. God is the God of explosive power and surprising love. If we affirm this to be the case, then his Word may just be as explosive as himself. Let it explode in your life. Read Scripture not for the only "true" meaning, but for the many jewels of insight that are packed into each story. Let it sink deeply into your soul and explode with new and deeper meanings. Realize that the Scriptures are alive with the glory of God.

What will be the result of letting Scripture explode? In Jesus' case, Mark tells us, "The large crowd was listening to him with delight" (12:37). First, they were delighted because Jesus had "upstaged" the scribes in their area of expertise, just as he had done previously to the Sadducees. It is reminiscent of Socrates' confounding the leading citizens of Athens and the young people taking delight in his difficult questions.

Second, the crowd may have listened in delight because *they* instinctively knew that life was more complex than the simple explanations of the scribes. People don't need to be "protected" from reality by well-meaning scribes, ancient or modern, who try to reconcile all discordant passages and explain God in neatly consistent ways. Control of the Scriptures, by the single-explanation concept, is largely an illusion. So let the Scripture come alive for you again. Let the Bible explode in your life. As you master it, let it master you. You will never have such security in God as when you realize you can't control God. And you will never feel that you understand Scripture so fully as when you let it explode beyond your control. These are paradoxes worthy of Jesus, who is both Lord and Son.

Dear Jesus, what am I mastered by? Am I mastered by the television control surfing the channels? Am I mastered by trying to gain more status and security in the world? Am I mastered by my passions and my lusts? What am I mastered by? Lord I read scripture and I know that it is truth. I know that you read scripture and dwelt on scripture and that you allowed the scripture to master every action, every move, and every thought in your life. I desire to have the scriptures master me. Master my passions, influence my thinking, and guide my actions. You loved the scriptures Lord Jesus. There you found consolation, revelation, and truth. Help me to love the scriptures that it would master my life and have an impact on my actions. Thank you Lord Jesus. Amen.

4

JESUS AND THE LIFE OF PRAYER

At the still point of the turning world . . . At the still point,
there the dance is . . . Except for the point, the still point,
There would be no dance, and there is only the dance.

—T. S. Eliot, *Four Quartets*

The practice of prayer is a standing rebuke to the wisdom of the world. The practice of prayer affirms a dimension to life that is unseen and unmeasurable, while the wisdom of the world considers something important only if it is visible and quantifiable. The practice of prayer proclaims that people are spiritual beings, rooted in the heart, while the wisdom of the world assumes that we are economic beings, concerned primarily with our personal net worth and an adequate retirement income. The practice of prayer indicates that God is the watcher, guide and protector of our lives, while the wisdom of the world teaches that unless *we* stand up for ourselves, no one will. The practice of prayer proves that "nothing will be impossible with God" (Luke 1:37), while the wisdom of the world says we need all the resources ahead of time and all the right people speaking up for us or we will not be able to get what we want in life. The practice of prayer says, "Don't worry." The wisdom of the world says, "Calculate."

Prayer is one of the principal ways of enlarging our awareness of God and of the universe. Prayer assumes there is more to the world than we can experience with our five senses. The great

77

diversity of living things in the world should not only increase our sense of wonder, but also give us an awareness of our human limitations. Michael Johnson may be the fastest sprinter, but he is slow compared with a dog, a horse or a cheetah. We may marvel at someone's hearing range, but it is nothing compared to the hearing ability of a number of animals. We bring in special dogs to crime scenes to pick up the scent of the suspected criminal because our human sense of smell is so feeble. The limits we experience should make us yearn for ways to explore the "spectrum of the soul" that is uniquely ours. Just as it is true that blind people often develop superior senses of hearing and deaf people have refined senses of touch, so should we compensate for our physical limitations by heightening our spiritual capacities, our sense of God. We spend hours at the "Y" trying to hone our limited physical capabilities; why not spend some concentrated effort attempting to strengthen our spiritual endowments?

Prayer is the unique opportunity which God gives us to develop a deeper understanding of Him and of the world. On one occasion Jesus chided the people for their shallowness of spiritual awareness:

> He also said to the crowds, "When you see a cloud rising in the west, you immediately say, 'It is going to rain'; and so it happens. And when you see the south wind blowing, you say, 'There will be scorching heat'; and it happens. You hypocrites! You know how to interpret the appearance of earth and sky, but why do you not know how to interpret the present time?" (Luke 12:54–56).

Jesus found fault with this crowd because their skill at "spiritual meteorology" did not compare with their ability to predict a coming storm.

Three Characteristics of Prayer

What is the essential nature of prayer? First, prayer is the *door* or *threshold* to the spiritual world where God dwells in unapproachable light. It is also the door to the inner world of the heart, whose contours have never fully been mapped. Prayer is the means to a "cartography of the soul," to a process of spiritual mapmaking. When we pray, we pursue Jesus into the deep things of life, where light and darkness dwell together and neither fully extinguishes the other. Prayer is the door into understanding the heavenly realms as well as the inky abyss. It opens new realms to us.

Prayer is also the *anchor* of our lives. It not only opens new vistas into the spiritual life, but also ties us ever more firmly to God in the process. One summer during college I worked at a large office building in San Francisco next to where a skyscraper was being built. It took the crew weeks just to drive the pilings deep into the ground. I still remember the ear-splitting crashes of hammers, the rush of pressurized air and the shouts of workers. They were anchoring the building, now among the tallest in San Francisco, deep into the bowels of the earth so that not even a major earthquake would topple the building. Prayer is like that. It anchors us to God by blasting through all our layers of debris and dirt so we might have a sturdy and strong life.

Prayer is, finally, a process of *working the earth of the heart,* as the ancient monastic writers might say. In her recent book, *The Cloister Walk,* Protestant author Kathleen Norris writes about the ways the Catholic monastic tradition provides a rhythm and depth for spirituality that most Protestants have never explored. When she says that the life of prayer works "the earth of the heart," she means that prayer is like the act of cultivation. In order to cultivate the soil, one must break up the hardened dirt clods, water the ground, free it from weeds and then plant a crop. Prayer is the way to "loosen up" the heart. During the natural course of our lives the "earth of our hearts" becomes parched, weed-infested and hard as flint. Unless we take care to break it up, to run our fingers again through the rich soil that we know is there, our lives become as destitute and as desiccated as a desert.

Jesus and Prayer

Prayer is the means Jesus used to open himself to God, to anchor himself to his Father and to work the earth of his heart. Jesus prayed often and taught his disciples to pray. Prayer was as necessary to him as the air he breathed. I believe it was prayer that gave Jesus his powerful sense of awareness and insight into people and the world. It connected him to God, the source of life, and he began to see things so much from the divine perspective that he had no doubt that his work was God's work. The practice of prayer gave Jesus an intuitive grasp of the truths of life as well as the political and religious realities around him. He could, figuratively speaking, see into another person's heart because he knew both his own heart and the heart of God. He could read the pulse of the culture with as much authority as a doctor can read someone's blood pressure.

It is my opinion that Jesus' ability to have a "sense" of things, to grasp the truths of life and of society, is available to us as well. It was not as if Jesus switched on a "divine power pack" and was suddenly able to see things, like Superman using his X-ray vision. I believe Jesus' ability was a human awareness cultivated through his constant practice of prayer. We should not simply read about Jesus and say, "What a rare and tremendous gift that *he* had!" That would be analogous to being awestruck "fans." We should, rather, yearn to imitate him and develop a similar commitment to prayer for ourselves. We should look at Jesus' life as testimony to the benefits of developing a life of prayer. Jesus invites us, through prayer, to experience new, fresh, deep, true and permanent insights into the nature of God, the world and the culture in which we live.

Most studies focus on prayer as a form of communication. Indeed, one of the earliest and briefest definitions of prayer I remember learning is "Prayer is talking with God." This definition is useful as far as it stresses our personal relationship with God and the ease of access we have to God. However, if we look at prayer primarily as a conversation, we might eventually perceive it as something that is "request-driven" and "answer-oriented." We limit prayer if we consider it a transaction where we "pay" with our words and God "gives over" the answer in response to our payment. Though supplication is certainly important, prayer is more a process of listening than of speaking; more an act of developing insight than seeking answers; more a dance with God than a talk with him.

In the rest of this chapter I will examine three aspects of prayer in Jesus' life: *quiet listening, simple acceptance,* and *earnest request.* I will close the chapter with some thoughts on the transformative power of prayer. My hope is that your perspective on prayer will be enlarged and your heart stimulated as you make the practice of prayer the foundation of your life.

Prayer as Quiet Listening

A verse I have loved for years comes from a psalm that is anything but quiet. Psalm 107 tells the story of distress and salvation of the people of Israel. It is a very rhythmic psalm that, over and over, relates the distress, outcry, deliverance, and praise of the people of God. The fourth stanza (verses 23–32) refers to salvation from stormy seas. The seas rage, the people cry to the Lord and the Lord delivers them. I like verse 50: "Then they were glad because they had quiet." Every time I read that psalm, I pause at the word "quiet." When I think about the contrast between the roaring of the seas and the peace of deliverance, I long for the quiet that the verse describes.

So much of life is not quiet. Life is torn by demands, and quiet is pushed aside, dispensed with, or otherwise lost. So many of us identify with Job who said in the midst of disaster:

> Truly the thing that I fear comes upon me, and what I dread befalls me.
> I am not at ease, nor am I quiet; I have no rest; but trouble comes (Job 3:25–26).

We live restless lives. Unquiet lives. In Pascal's words, we lead lives of "quiet desperation." How can we transform each day into a time of quiet *listening?*

Jesus felt the need for quiet prayer and listening throughout his life. Consider the following passages:

In the morning, while it was still very dark, he got up and went out to a deserted place, and there he prayed (Mark 1:35).

But now more than ever the word about Jesus spread abroad; many crowds would gather to hear him and to be cured of their diseases. But he would withdraw to deserted places and pray (Luke 5:15–16).

Now during those days he went out to the mountain to pray; and he spent the night in prayer to God. And when day came, he called his disciples and chose twelve of them, whom he also named apostles (Luke 6:12–13).

Now about eight days after these sayings Jesus took with him Peter and John and James, and went up on the mountain to pray (Luke 9:28).

When he reached [the Mount of Olives], he said to them, "Pray that you may not come into the time of trial." Then he withdrew from them about a stone's throw, knelt down, and prayed (Luke 22:40–41).

Why did Jesus desire quiet? Because he needed the things that only quiet could bring. He needed the opportunity to listen to God and to his own heart. His times of prayer are mentioned during his life transitions and pressing activities. These were times when he needed to "collect" or "center" himself. He lived his entire life before God, yet he needed the refreshment of soul that only quiet listening could bring.

More specifically, what did Jesus seek during his times of quiet listening? Four words that capture Jesus' need are *balance, rhythm, harmony,* and *integrity.* A brief thought on each will help us understand the essence of quiet listening.

Jesus' search for *balance* in his life is evident in the passage from Mark 1, quoted above. He had spent the day healing "all who were sick or possessed with demons" (Mark 1:32). The next day looked to be equally busy, so before dawn he retreated to a deserted place. He needed time to restore his soul, to cultivate the deep springs of life, to drink deeply from the rivers of life in a desert place.

I used to think establishing balance meant eliminating the competing forces tugging at you. If you had balance, I thought, you would sail through life with ease. I now believe that balance is a creative state where opposing forces still tug on you, and often threaten to pull you apart, but are mastered by the force of something greater in your life. This something greater, for Jesus, was the reality of God's presence.

Several years ago I taught my daughter how to ride a bike. It was almost as painful for me as for her. She would fall, scrape her knees, cry and say that she really never wanted to learn to ride. But one day everything clicked and she finally rode without falling. I watched her pedal off that day and felt a mixture of the fear and admiration parents have when their children ride into the next stage of independence. I saw her almost fall to the right, then correct herself and almost fall to the left and then establish something of a balance as she teetered down the road. My daughter was able to achieve "balance" when she learned to remain upright in spite of the competing forces which tugged at her on either side. Maintaining balance is keeping your center amid competing demands. Jesus learned this balance through his times of quiet listening.

Jesus also sought the proper *rhythm* in life. We perform well when we are "in sync" and moving well with the flow of the day. We all seek a steady "beat" in our lives, so that our pulse throbs with the pulse of the universe, with the pulse of God.

A few years ago a television announcer was interviewing Michael Jordan, star guard of the Chicago Bulls. Michael had played below his standards in the first quarter, but then had recovered and finished with a very strong game. When the announcer asked him how his game changed between the first and second quarters, Jordan said, "I let the game come to me, rather than trying to impose my will on the game." What Jordan meant, in our language, is that he perceived the "flow" or the rhythm of the game and adjusted his own inner clock to merge with it. He was trying too hard at first; when he relaxed and "let the game come to him," he was able to play at his normal level of excellence.

Perceiving the rhythms of life is in large part an intuitive exercise. One senses or feels the essence of what is happening and tries to become a part of it. Jesus already knew his call and the basic contours of his life, but what he needed to determine was the timing for his life. He knew it was not the right time to ask for authority over the kingdoms of the world; he knew it was not time to charge into Jerusalem. But what *was* it the right time to do? By quiet listening in prayer, Jesus was able to develop a relaxed and accepting approach to the timetable of God.

Jesus also sought *harmony* during his times of quiet listening. When I speak of harmony, I think of a jazz band. Each instrument is distinctive, but the blended sound touches the deep chords of life. By itself, a drum, bass, trombone, or saxophone can be a searching and inspiring instrument. But when combined with all the others, they produce a fullness of sound, a symphonic plenitude that calms the soul. Jesus desired harmony between himself and God, himself and others. He prayed all night before selecting the disciples in order to achieve such a union of wills with God that it would become clear whom to choose. I believe the result of his all-night prayer session was not a list of names, but rather a heart so attuned to the will and purposes of God that he could be sure whom to select when confronted by various people the next day.

The fact that Jesus spent the entire night praying before a big decision tells us something about the function of solitude in his life. Jesus fought the big battles of life in solitude. We tend to think battles are fought on the battlefield, whether an athletic arena, workplace, boardroom, classroom, or home. But Jesus demonstrated that the battle begins *before* the actual physical encounter takes place. The real battle takes place in silence, when you are alone, as you seek to attune yourself to the will of God.

Applying this insight to modern life, I would say that the sale does not take place with the client, but in the quiet of your heart the night before. The class doesn't begin when the students enter the classroom, but when you work through the issues in the dark hours. The interview is not a success when it is being conducted, but when you are alone and affirm your value as a person and potential employee. Preparing for these events requires more than simply going over a set of notes; it involves seeking a harmony, a blending of wills, a union of hearts that will assure the outcome even before the event takes place.

One of the best teachers I ever knew, a professor of ancient philosophy, used to excuse himself from a meeting at least an hour before any lecture he was scheduled to give. All he would say, with a smile, was, "I must go contemplate the Forms." The secret of his dynamism was his awareness that greatness was nurtured in silence.

The word that sums up the entire phenomenon of quiet listening is *integrity*—a sense of wholeness, fullness or completeness. Jesus' integrity is reflected in his words when he first met Nathanael. All Jesus said was, "Here is truly an Israelite in whom there is no deceit" (John 1:47). A person of integrity recognizes that same trait in another person. Jesus sought to "integrate" his life so that he would be an "integer." He would be one self, one with God and one with humankind, fully divine and fully human, fully able to bear the burden of our sin.

Quiet listening need not be limited to times of retreat and solitude. I have discovered that certain activities can aid us in our listening. I believe that each person needs a particular activity, unrelated to his or her call or work, which provides an opportunity for quiet listening. A pastor friend of mine spends several hours each week painting toy soldiers. His hobby is painstaking and slow, but he always rises refreshed, with new insights about life flowing from his lips.

I have found that gardening is a rewarding activity for me. I take pride in digging up ground and preparing it for planting, leaving the actual planting and cultivation to others. As my hands become dirty, my soul becomes purer.

I see the tangled root system of the plants and I wonder about the tangled nature of our lives. I think deeply about families I know who have fallen apart, people who are immobilized because of the complexities of life, the insolvable issues in my own life.

I work the soil, breaking up clods of dirt, removing weeds, mingling the light dry topsoil with the fresh damp soil beneath and thinking about how the "earth of our hearts" needs to be broken up, watered and mixed with fresh, rich dirt from the depths. I see healthy plants and I see weeds, and I count many more of the latter than the former. Seeing how the weeds seem to grow quicker and sturdier, I think about the nature of the world and see how every new invention, the latest being the Internet, offers so many good plantings, but also many more weeds. These are some of the lessons of life that come as a result of my quiet but active listening in my garden. Without quiet listening we are unable to hear the voice of God. Jesus needed this time; how much more do we?

Simple Acceptance

Though much time in prayer is quiet listening, some part should include learning to practice simple acceptance. A wonderful example of simple acceptance is the response of Mary, after hearing from the angel Gabriel that she would bear the baby Jesus: "Here am I, the servant of the Lord; let it be with me according to your word" (Luke 1:38). She accepted the Word of God and the will of God, simply and briefly.

Simple acceptance must be differentiated from grim resignation. Resignation is going along with something because it is useless to fight it. Resignation and resentment often travel together, and they look for opportunities to rear their heads and assert their wills. Simple acceptance is different. It emerges from a realization that what is being asked of you, or required of you, is really a good thing even though the full extent of its "goodness" might not be clear. You accept it as good because the person requesting your acceptance is good. You are convinced this person has your best interests at heart. Simple acceptance to the will and Word of God says, "Here am I; send me!" (Isa. 6:8); or "Speak, Lord, for your servant is listening" (1 Sam. 3:10); or "Not what I want, but what you want" (Mark 14:36); or even, "It is good for me that I was humbled, so that I might learn your statutes" (Ps. 119:71). The sentiment is reflected in the well-known hymn:

> In simple trust like those who heard
> Beyond the Syrian sea,
> The gracious calling of the Lord,
> Let us like them without a word,
> Rise up and follow thee.

Simple acceptance must also be distinguished from passivity. An accepting heart may also be on fire for social justice or political involvement. Simple acceptance is a matter of balance. One struggle of life is knowing what to accept and what to resist. The Serenity Prayer, attributed to theologian Reinhold Niebuhr, asks God to grant us the serenity to accept the things we cannot change, the courage to change the things we can and the wisdom to know the difference. What a good description of the balance we need to seek! To practice simple acceptance is to gratefully and willingly embrace the unchangeable realities of the world without giving up hope for a better day in the future.

Reaching a point of simple acceptance can be a process of *struggle.* One of the best biblical illustrations of this is provided by the patriarch Abraham. He was promised a child by God as early as Genesis 12. Years passed and the child had not come when God reaffirmed the promise in Genesis 15, so Abraham protested. "O Lord God, what will you give me, for I continue childless?" (Gen. 15:2) After further discussion, where God repeated the promise, Abraham accepted God's Word simply. "He believed the Lord; and the Lord reckoned it to him as righteousness" (Gen. 15:6). Abraham got to a point of simple acceptance, but not without some initial doubts and questioning.

Simple acceptance also means a commitment to live in the present. This may seem obvious, but many times our lives become dominated by regrets over the past or hopes for the future. The great seventeenth-century thinker, Blaise Pascal, reflecting on this problem, said the pain of the human condition is that "we never live, but only hope to live." But God is the great I AM. His eternal presence can be seen in the following anonymous poem:

> "My name is I am." He paused
> I waited. He continued,
> "When you live in the past,
> with its mistakes and regrets,
> it is hard. I am not there.
> My name is not I was.
>
> When you live in the future,
> with its problems and fears,
> it is hard. I am not there.
> My name is not I will be.
>
> When you live in this moment,
> it is not hard. I am here.
> My name is I am."

Jesus practiced simple acceptance throughout his life. It is evident in the Lord's prayer when he taught his disciples to say, "Your kingdom come. Your will be done, on earth as it is in heaven" (Matt. 6:10). Perhaps even more evident is his prayer after the seventy disciples had returned from their mission. In a moment of gratitude, Jesus prayed:

I thank you, Father, Lord of heaven and earth, because you have hidden these things from the wise and the intelligent and have revealed them to infants; yes, Father, for such was your gracious will (Luke 10:21).

The prayer is brief, simple, confident and grateful. Jesus is grateful for the wisdom of God which reveals truth to the unwise, grateful that he knows God, grateful that God's involvement in the world is gracious. It is the prayer of a person who has learned the secret of simple acceptance.

Earnest Request

Asking and receiving in prayer is a theme that runs throughout Jesus' teaching. Here are just a couple of examples:

> Ask, and it will be given you; search, and you will find; knock, and the door will be opened for you. For everyone who asks receives (Matt. 7:7–8).

> Very truly, I tell you, if you ask anything of the Father in my name, he will give it to you. Until now you have not asked for anything in my name. Ask and you will receive, so that your joy may be complete (John 16:23–24).

Sometimes statements like this are qualified a bit with a reminder to ask in faith (Mark 11:24) or to abide in Jesus when asking (John 15:7), but often the emphasis remains on asking and receiving. These promises have frequently led to more pain than pleasure. Sometimes Christians tend to develop a view of God as a "genie" to be summoned in times of need. Other times we are confused when our requests apparently fall on deaf ears. Perhaps, we think, God has promised too much, has "overplayed his hand."

We will be less likely to feel that God has let us down or is deaf to our pleas if we understand that requesting favors is only one aspect of prayer. Prayer as *earnest request* is more a desire to change *us* than to change our circumstances, more a desire to seek communion *with* God than things *from* God, more a process of accepting things than desiring things. Yet since we are encouraged to take our requests to God, in this brief section I will look at two aspects of asking in prayer: *orderly* asking and *shameless* asking.

An example of *orderly* asking is Jesus' model of prayer provided for his disciples. The Lord's Prayer appears twice in the

Bible (Matt. 6:9–13 and Luke 11:2–4). Jesus contrasts this prayer with the long-winded and showy prayers of the hypocrites. Note its simplicity:

> Our Father in heaven,
> hallowed be your name.
> Your kingdom come.
> Your will be done,
> on earth as it is in heaven.
> Give us this day our daily bread.
> And forgive us our debts,
> as we also have forgiven our debtors.
> And do not bring us to the time of trial
> but rescue us from the evil one (Matt. 6:9–13).

The Lord's Prayer teaches us that prayer can have a form. There is a way to pray, a technique to it. It is a great comfort to realize this. Many of us, brought up in traditions that emphasize spontaneous prayer, are afraid to pray in public for fear that we will utter such distracting or bland prayers that people will be more embarrassed than blessed. We become free when we realize we can use words of others to shape our own prayers.

I am convinced one of the reasons the religion of Islam is making such advances in the world today is that it provides its adherents not simply the form and words for prayer, but also the various *postures* to assume while praying. People appreciate specifics.

The Lord's Prayer not only gives us precise words to pray, but also provides a form that we can use in prayer. Start with adoration, continue with confession of one's sin, make requests, and end with an ascription of praise to God. Even in the brevity of the Lord's Prayer, asking is only a small part of the whole. The greater emphasis is on giving glory to God.

Realize too that the Lord's Prayer is only one of many prayers in the Scripture. The Old Testament provides several examples of heartfelt prayer which appear to follow certain forms that we may find useful. (See, for example, Daniel 9:4–19 or 1 Kings 8:22–53.)

Learning some set formulas for prayer can be liberating. When I was preparing to go to Honduras for a mission trip in 1996, I spent some intensive effort in regaining my conversational Spanish skills. What I found most helpful was memorizing a number of sentences that would frequently be used as greetings or basic questions. By learning these questions word for word, I was better able to meet people, to engage them in conversation, and to comprehend deeper levels of communication than I would if I hadn't become comfortable with some of the basic phrases. Learning some of the "mechanics" or "techniques" of prayer—phrases of praise, how to confess sins, how to ask for a need, how to thank God for blessings—can be a milestone in one's spiritual development.

The idea of *shameless* prayer comes from a passage in Luke directly after Jesus gave the Lord's Prayer.

> [Jesus] said to them, "Suppose one of you has a friend, and you go to him at midnight and say to him, 'Friend, lend me three loaves of bread; for a friend of mine has arrived, and I have nothing to set before him.' And he answers from within, 'Do not bother me; the door has already been locked, and my children are with me in bed; I cannot get up and give you anything.' I tell you, even though he will not get up and give him anything because he is his friend, at least because of his persistence he will get up and give him whatever he needs (Luke 11:5–8).

The word translated "persistence" in the last sentence has also been translated as "importunity" *(Revised Standard Version)* or "boldness" *(New International Version)*. Perhaps these translations are all trying to soften the Greek word, which is literally rendered "shamelessness" or "without shame." In other passages, Jesus talks about the value of *persistent* prayer (Luke 18:1–8), but here the emphasis is on shameless, brazen, impudent or brash prayer. Jesus assures us that sincere prayers, from the very orderly to the very shameless, will be heard *and answered* by God. By translating the word literally as "shameless," it actually provides more of a comfort than by taking refuge behind the less emphatic words "persistence" or "boldness."

But what does Jesus mean by shameless prayer, and why would he commend it? First, a few comments on the word. Synonyms for *shameless* include *boldfaced, brash, or impudent.* A shameless person is one who robs a house and returns to ask if he can wipe away traces of his fingerprints. A shameless salesman is one who sells you a defective car and then refuses to have it fixed but, instead, tries to sell you another one. Shameless behavior is insulting and inappropriate.

How does shamelessness relate to prayer? For a long time I felt they had no relationship, until I heard an interview with a pastor on a cable television station. She was telling about a serious one-car accident while traveling with her son. She was relatively unhurt, but her son was bleeding profusely and was seriously injured. While she drove to the hospital, she began to pray. She was surprised at the tone of her prayer. Rather than using an imploring tone, she began to speak in a demanding, commanding tone. She remembers screaming at God, ordering him, forbidding him to let her son die. She said things like, "God, you have *no right* to do this to *my* son. You are *not* going to let him die. Make him well!" She was brazen, demanding, dry-eyed and volatile. She was also utterly shameless. Her son lived.

Why would God ever hear and answer such a shameless, desperate prayer? A clue may be found in the closing chapter of the Book of Job. When God finally spoke to Job and his friends, after several chapters of frustrating silence, God rebuked Job's friends and commended Job:

> My wrath is kindled against you [Eliphaz] and against your two friends; for you have not spoken of me what is right, as my servant Job has (Job 42:7).

Keep in mind that throughout the Book of Job, Job had been saying the most nasty things about God. He said things about God that most people wouldn't say about bitter foes. Yet as the book concludes, God commends Job for speaking "what is right." Something in the character of God honors the heartfelt cry of the desperate heart more than the outwardly pious, correct, dignified words of the defenders of God who feel little genuine emotion. God, frankly, can take care of his own defense. He knows a shameless cry often reflects the true depths of the human heart. Wherever you are on the spectrum of despair, from a life that is ordered and relatively calm to one driven by the most hellish desperation, you can be sure that God hears and answers. As if to underscore this point in the Gospel of Luke, note the verse following the story of the shameless man:

> So I say to you, Ask, and it will be given you; search, and you will find; knock, and the door will be opened for you. For everyone who asks receives (Luke 11:9–10).

The Transformative Power of Prayer

I once had a pastor with a sign on his desk that said, simply, "Prayer changes things." After more than twenty years of thinking about that brief sentence, I believe I would say it differently. I would say, "Prayer changes *us*." The ultimate value of prayer is that it opens us to understand God and the world in fresh ways. Prayer gives us new spectacles to see the world—glasses that put the seemingly huge demands of contemporary life in a new perspective. Prayer helps us listen to the voice of God, accept the will of God and ask for the good things of God.

One experience of Jesus that shows the transformative power of prayer was the Transfiguration (Matt. 17:1–8; Mark 9:2–8; Luke 9:28–36). I only need to quote the first few verses in Luke's account to illustrate the main point:

> Now about eight days after these sayings Jesus took with him Peter and John and James, and went up on the mountain to pray. And while he was praying, the appearance of his face changed, and his clothes became dazzling white. Suddenly they saw two men, Moses and Elijah, talking to him. They appeared

in glory and were speaking of his departure, which he was about to accomplish at Jerusalem (Luke 9:28–31).

Two dimensions of our ordinary existence are space and time. We are in one and only one place at any given time. We cannot go back or forward in time. We can only imagine a conversation with great figures from the past.

In the passage just quoted, Jesus' space and time are *changed* as a result of prayer. The change of space was reflected by his altered countenance and clothes. Luke stresses that it was *while he was praying* that the appearance of his face changed. Prayer either released a tremendous energy or caught him up to a new reality in such a way that his face and clothes were transformed. The biblical picture that lies behind this experience is that of Moses when he came down Mount Sinai after receiving the tablets of the law from God (Ex. 34:29–35).

> As he came down from the mountain with the two tablets of the covenant in his hand, Moses did not know that the skin of his face shown because he had been talking with God (verse 29).

When the people of Israel saw Moses' face shining, they were afraid and asked him to wear a veil when talking to them. In Luke's account, *Jesus* is the one whose face becomes transformed and whose garments shine. Whether the garments themselves change color or the lightning-like shine comes from the body of Jesus is unimportant. The point is that through the intimacy of prayer, Jesus' physical condition is changed. He becomes a partaker of the heavenly realm; he receives a foretaste of the heavenly banquet. The Apostle Paul, thinking about this passage and the story of Moses coming down the mountain, holds out hope that the same thing will happen for all Christians:

> All of us, with unveiled faces, seeing the glory of the Lord as though reflected in a mirror, are being transformed into the same image from one degree of glory to another; for this comes from the Lord, the Spirit (2 Cor. 3:18).

But Jesus' experience of prayer also transcended the human category of *time*. While he was praying, Moses and Elijah appeared, representing the Law and the Prophets. They spoke with him about his "departure" in Jerusalem. The scene is reminiscent of the movie *Field of Dreams,* where Kevin Costner, James Earl Jones and others are transported through time to meet Shoeless Joe Jackson and other baseball legends from 1920. In this case, Moses had to "come forward" 1200 years and Elijah more than 800, in order to speak with Jesus.

The important thing to notice here is that prayer was the means for transforming space and time. In this regard, prayer becomes something like a dance. Devotees of dance point to it as the primary human activity through which people are seemingly able to be transcend the present realm of space and time. Dancers have a sense that they are in their own world— a world of less structure and different rules. The electricity of prayer, of the dance, was evident on the Mount of Transfiguration. Jesus was changed, and the rules of space and time no longer applied to him. Let us also behold the glory of the Lord in prayer. I can't promise your countenance will change or your garments will shine, or if you will have conversations with important figures of the past. I do know, however, that you can be changed, and the change will be good, fulfilling and radiantly memorable.

Jesus Christ, my Lord, how you loved to pray. I read where you would spend time in solitude, reflecting, meditating, and thinking about your Father. You engaged your mind, your spirit, and your heart in deep communication with the one whom you loved. Lord Jesus, out of prayer you found your center, you found your source of strength, and you found your direction for the day. Out of prayer, you sensed anew the will of God. You prayed with such passion that even the disciples asked that you would teach them to pray. Your mind stayed focused and your heart reflected deeply upon God. When I pray Jesus, I find the opposite with the phone ringing, with my daily planner filled with appointments that cry out for attention in the course of the day. I am laden with past failures and emotional blockage. Jesus, I want to pray like you. I want to learn how to pray. I want to understand that prayer is an essential part of my inner life. And when I pray, I want to reflect and think about you and the way you prayed with passion and the way you sought the Father's will. Jesus, teach me to pray that I might have an awareness of God. Teach me to pray, that I might have patience. Teach me to pray that I might catch a glimpse of your grace in my life. Teach me to pray that my heart would burn with passion and my life would reflect the values of God. Amen.

5

JESUS AND THE FOCUSED LIFE

We must be still and still moving Into another intensity
For a further union, a deeper communion Through the dark
cold and the empty desolation. . . .

—T. S. Eliot, *Four Quartets*

After each movement of a symphony, the orchestra stops to retune. After almost every glance through the binoculars, one must refocus. Each time the ball touches the dirt in a professional baseball game, the umpire must examine and clean it. Why? Because even when we use things as intended we change them and make them less perfect, less able to perform the work they were designed for. The use of a thing distorts or damages it.

So it is with our lives. The more we live, even in ways that are healthy, the more we need to recharge our batteries, reclaim our first love, recover our focus. Nothing stays in focus forever, and our lives are no exception. We lose focus for a number of reasons. We become distracted by the noise and the clutter of life. We become buried under an avalanche of words and information, and feel curiously weakened rather than strengthened by so much data. We become preoccupied by so many worries about family, finances, health, and the future. Endless thinking about these things corrodes hope and takes away joy.

Often the process of growing up is a process of losing focus rather than gaining it. A friend in his forties told me he had only recently rediscovered the sense of clarity and vision he had felt as an eighteen year old. For more than twenty-five years he had lost his focus. He is a Roman Catholic and during high school he planned to study the life and theology of St. Augustine, one of the great thinkers of the Christian church. In order to do this, he was told he must master Latin and then Greek. He needed to study the history of ancient philosophy, paying special attention to the Platonic tradition since Augustine's work was indebted to the Platonists and neo-Platonists. In addition, he probably should study contemporary philosophy to understand how philosophers currently frame issues and problems. What began as a love for Augustine soon became so clouded by the pressures of learning other "necessary" disciplines that my friend lost his motivation. Good things had crowded out the best thing for him. Only recently has he rediscovered his focus on Augustine, and soon plans to publish an entire book on just one chapter of Augustine's *Confessions*. He has now returned to his love and focus of 1970.

My own pilgrimage has been somewhat similar. During my freshman year at college my heart was set afire by the Scriptures. I studied them, memorized them, taught them, wrote about them, and spent a good deal of my waking hours thinking about them. I neglected other studies so I could immerse myself in them. I decided to get an advanced degree in Biblical Studies so I could dive still deeper into the sacred pages. That decision precipitated my loss of focus. In order to get my doctorate in Biblical Studies, I had to spend hundreds of hours studying ancient and modern languages, theories of religion, Judaism, Hellenistic philosophy and religion, sociology of religion and history of the interpretation of the Bible. The fire I had for the Scriptures, the focus that first riveted me, gradually subsided. Study of the Bible became a chore, and reading and writing scholarly articles drained my energy. It was not until I began to study the Bible for spiritual nurture, rather than academic advancement, that it again became alive to me.

The goal of this chapter is to show how Jesus maintained his focus in life and how he continued to keep the vision alive which had been given him at his baptism. How did Jesus maintain the freshness of his faith, the utter commitment to his call-ing? What was the secret to his ability to stay focused on his work? And what might we learn from Jesus about maintain-ing our own focus in life?

We need to begin by making a distinction between focus and preoccupation. My nine-year-old son is preoccupied with the National Basketball Association. All he thinks about is play-ing professional basketball when he gets older. In a recent NBA draft seven of the early draft choices were either recent high school graduates or college underclassmen. Some were going to the NBA even before their 20th birthday. My son couldn't sleep that night. The next morning he told me he was reeval-uating his future and wasn't sure whether he would go directly to the NBA from high school or college! My son has a pre-occupation, but it is probably not a focus.

A preoccupation is something that demands all of a person's attention right now, but a focus, in our use of the term, is a longer-term interest similar to a call or mission in life. A pre-occupation is temporary and never leaves one's mind for long, while a focus may, at times, slip from our consciousness. A pre-occupation carries with it a sort of desperation, but a focus puts our hearts at ease. A focus enables us to establish a rhythm, a balance, a harmony and integrity with ourselves and life. A focus may be all-consuming, but it normally allows us to live a full and balanced life.

So, to repeat our previous questions, how did Jesus main-tain his focus in life? How did he keep the fire of his early call kindled? What made him stay the course when the distrac-tions, temptations, and opposition to him became so monu-mental? I want to examine not so much the things that fed his soul in these times (such as prayer and the Scriptures), but how he came to a knowledge of the *message* and *mission* which guided him until the end of his life. Jesus was ultimately sus-tained by the power of God. But there were also identifiable factors which helped him maintain and refine his focus in life.

The primary factor in enabling him to maintain his focus in life was his ability to achieve *clarity on his message and mission.*

This clarity was something that grew and was refined in the crucible of Jesus' life.

Clarity of Message

Ever since the first sermon Jesus gave at his home synagogue (Luke 4:16–30) in which he alienated his hearers, he was reaching for clarity in his message. In that sermon he quoted Isaiah 61:1–2 and then said, "Today this scripture has been fulfilled in your hearing" (Luke 4:21). The two main points from the Isaiah quotation that would be fulfilled in his ministry were the work of proclamation ("to proclaim the year of the Lord's favor" [verse 19]) and the work of healing ("recovery of sight to the blind, to let the oppressed go free"[verse 18]). Jesus would formulate and articulate his message within these broad biblical categories of proclamation and healing. In the next several pages, I will discuss one significant aspect of Jesus' message: the centrality of *mercy*.

The Quality of Mercy

Several Greek words in the Gospels can be translated as "compassion" or "mercy." As nouns the words suggest the idea of pity or sympathy to the unfortunate or needy. The verb translated "to have compassion" literally means to "pour out one's insides" for another person. My perspective is that Jesus' emphasis on mercy arises out of his encounter with life and not simply from his reading the Scriptures or meditating on his call.

Jesus spent a good deal of time at the beginning of his ministry healing people. He healed lepers, those who were possessed with demons and "any who were sick with various kinds of diseases" (Luke 4:40).

Responding to the immediate demands of human need seemed to drive Jesus' early ministry. Word of his healing power soon spread throughout the countryside and he was besieged by the crowds. Jesus could not stay and heal all the people who presented themselves to him. He needed to go to other cities and proclaim the kingdom of God. So instead of healing everyone, Jesus developed the doctrine of compassion or mercy which could guide the disciples' actions.

Jesus' "doctrine of mercy" became clear in the story of the healing of a man with a withered hand:

> On another Sabbath he entered the synagogue and taught, and there was a man there whose right hand was withered. The scribes and the Pharisees watched him to see whether he would cure on the Sabbath, so that they might find an accusation against him. Even though he knew what they were thinking, he said to the man who had the withered hand, "Come and stand here." He got up and stood there. Then Jesus said to them, "I ask you, is it lawful to do good or to do harm on the Sabbath, to save life or to destroy it?" After looking around at all of them, he said to him, "Stretch out your hand." He did so, and his hand was restored. But they were filled with fury and discussed with one another what they might do to Jesus" (Luke 6:6–11).

To understand this passage, we should realize that the Sabbath observance was one of the central religious practices in Judaism of Jesus' day. To keep the Sabbath loyally meant to refrain from work on that day. God rested from His work on the seventh day; his people were commanded to do the same. One Talmudic saying captures the importance of Sabbath observance perfectly: "If all Israel keeps Sabbath for only one day, Messiah will come."

But restrictions always invite questions. What did it mean to refrain from work? Did that limit how far one could walk on the Sabbath? What objects one could lift? Where one could go? Which activities must be avoided? By the time of Jesus more than thirty-five regulations were "on the books" regarding proper Sabbath observance.

Much of the antagonism of the religious leaders toward Jesus developed because of a difference of interpretation concerning which activities were permitted on the Sabbath. The Jewish law most crucial for understanding the controversies between Jesus and the religious authorities is: "Every case of danger of life allows for the suspension of the Sabbath" (Yoma 8.6—Mishnah). The implication is that nothing less than "danger of life" would justify working on the Sabbath.

We get to the nub of the controversy and the unfolding of Jesus' doctrine of mercy when we look at the question Jesus asks the religious authorities.

I ask you, is it lawful to do good or to do harm on the Sabbath, to save life or to destroy it? (Luke 6:9)

The form of the question is very important. For Jesus this was *one* question, while for the religious authorities it was *two*. The authorities would ask for clarification. If the person's or animal's life was not in danger, then it was not lawful to do good. So from the perspective of the religious leaders, one could not answer the question with a simple "yes" or "no." One must first know the condition of the sufferer.

Here is where Jesus differed from the religious authorities. For Jesus, the issue was not "danger of life" but the presence of human need. To "do good" and to "save life" were synonymous concepts for Jesus; by doing good he *was* saving life. To the religious authorities, a person was *not* doing good on the Sabbath if he was doing something that could just as easily be done the next day. Clearly, the man with the withered hand was not in danger of losing his life overnight. Therefore, in the Pharisees' understanding, Jesus should heal on the next day to avoid violating the commandment of God.

The fact that Jesus made "doing good" synonymous with "saving life" proved that a crucial feature of his ministry was to show mercy to people. He expanded the meaning of sabbath by declaring that any demonstration of human compassion was legitimate on that day. Such a statement not only determined the course of Jesus' ministry, but led to irrepressible conflict with the Jewish authorities.

Jesus' practice of healing in spite of the conflict it caused helped him refine his doctrine of mercy and his understanding of his primary message. Human need, on whatever day of the week, would take precedence over religious regulations. Doing good and saving life were the essence of the work of God. Those healed would remember with gratitude his touch, his words, and the immediate sense of strength returning to damaged limbs; the religious people would never forget Jesus' brazen defiance of Sabbath law as they interpreted it.

Jesus' acts of mercy sparked gratitude and hatred—plans to honor him as a king and to kill him as a religious transgressor. But even more importantly, his acts of mercy soon became a *central teaching* or *message* of his life. In the same chapter (Luke 6), Jesus gave his "Sermon on the Plain." The heart of that sermon focused on the law of love (6:27–36). It is interesting that the previous Sabbath healing seemed to form some of the background for this teaching, because the two groups of people we are challenged to love are our enemies (i.e., the religious leaders) and those who cannot pay us back (i.e., those who had been healed). Both groups are included in the next verse:

But love your enemies, do good, and lend, expecting nothing in return (verse 35).

The theme of the passage is stated clearly in verse 36:

Be merciful, just as your Father is merciful.

What God requires of disciples is merciful action. Acting mercifully requires imitating Jesus, who learned that healing and saving life were synonymous. It is always the right time to do good to people.

As if to drive home the importance of merciful action, Jesus models it again on a journey to the city of Nain with his disciples (Luke 7:11–17).

As he approached the gate of the town, a man who had died was being carried out. He was his mother's only son, and she was a widow (verse 12).

The situation is one of complete desperation. The woman was already a widow and therefore in a vulnerable situation in the society. Now that her son had died, she had lost her last shred of respect and dignity. The crowd that accompanied her in her grief (verse 11) would soon melt away, leaving her abandoned and helpless, cherishing fading memories as she attempted to adjust to her new life.

This was the situation encountered by Jesus and his disciples.

When the Lord saw her, he had compassion for her and said to her, "Do not weep." Then he came forward and touched the bier, and the bearers stood still. And he said, "Young man, I say to you, rise!" The dead man sat up and began to speak (Luke 7:13–15).

Jesus demonstrated compassion by restoring the son to the desperate widow. He had determined on that fateful Sabbath day to throw in his lot with the weak, sick, maimed and blind in life. He would give dead sons back to their weeping mothers; he would strengthen weak limbs; he would heal swirling minds and confused hearts. Compassion, showing mercy, "pouring out his insides" for others would be the central action of his life and a recurring theme of his teaching.

The verb meaning "to have pity" or "to have compassion" appears twice more in Luke's Gospel, in two of the most memorable of Jesus' parables. In the Parable of the Good Samaritan (10:29–37), Jesus contrasted the keep-your-distance attitude of religious purity practiced by the priest and Levite, who leave the half-dead man on the road without attending to his need, with the action of the Samaritan. Although Jews and Samaritans usually despised each other, note the behavior of *this* Samaritan:

A Samaritan while traveling came near him; and when he saw him, he was moved with pity. He went to him and bandaged his wounds, having poured oil and wine on them. Then he put him on his own animal, brought him to an inn, and took care of him (Luke 10:33–34).

It is interesting that the first person other than Jesus who is noted for compassion in Luke's Gospel is a Samaritan. He is the epitome of a neighbor because he demonstrated pity on one who was in need. Jesus' last words of the parable, "Go and do likewise," remind us that the essential rule of neighborly conduct is showing mercy.

Showing compassion is the *message* of Jesus; it is the *method* of Jesus; it is the action *commended* by Jesus. It is also the way that God acts, which is the point of the Parable of the Prodigal Son (Luke 15:11–32). The story is familiar, and we don't need to review the full text here. Suffice it to say that it is the story of two sons, the younger of whom demands his inheritance from the father and squanders it in riotous living in a far-off land. When the younger son "comes to himself" and realizes his condition, he resolves to return to his father. He prepares a confession: "Father, I have sinned against heaven and before you; I am no longer worthy to be called your son; treat me like one of your hired hands" (vverse 18–19). As he comes within view of his home, the father sees him. The text says:

> But while he was still far off, his father saw him and was filled with compassion; he ran and put his arms around him and kissed him (Luke 15:20).

There's that word *compassion* again. The father orders a banquet to be prepared for his long-lost son. Images of intimacy and haste tumble over each other as preparations are quickly made. The story shows that there is something close to recklessness about divine compassion, an audacious reaching out to redeem a son regardless of the costs or the social ramifications. Indeed, many people have noted that the elder son, who complained to his father about this lavish show of affection, had a valid point. In terms of strict justice, the father had been too lenient. But when compassion becomes the central virtue of life and the central value in faith, one might need to err on the side of mercy. So what if one cannot be paid back in full? So what if mercy has a high cost? So what if one is accused of unfairness? So what if one is ridiculed for "wasting" one's resources? As Jesus says, "Do good . . . expecting nothing in return" (Luke 6:35).

A final example of compassion occurs in a passage that doesn't use the word. The story is the healing of the centurion's servant (Luke 7:1–10). It demonstrates Jesus' compassion even when he is misunderstood and treated inappropriately. Jesus is in Capernaum when a centurion, a high-ranking officer in the Roman army, is in need:

> A centurion there had a slave whom he valued highly, and who was ill and close to death. When he heard about Jesus, he sent some Jewish elders to him, asking him to come and heal his slave (vverse 2–3).

Why didn't the centurion come to Jesus in person and request his presence? Because a centurion's life was centered around authority and the chain of command. As a senior officer in the best army in the Western world, considerations of rank precluded him from coming directly to Jesus. The way authority worked in his sphere was that he gave a command and his subordinates obeyed it; he assumed the Jews worked the same way. So he made a request to the Jewish leaders expecting them to "command" Jesus to do what he requested.

In addition, the centurion had done a favor for the Jews in the past by building their synagogue. They were indebted to him. Power works in society by way of IOUs. You do favors for people and later, in a time of need, you "call in those favors," from people who can help you. Now was the time to call in a favor, since a prized servant was at the point of death. "Get Jesus over here at once!"

Despite the fact that the centurion had misunderstood Jesus' relationship to the Jewish elders and had actually insulted him, Jesus went when they asked him (verse 6). Nothing is said about what was going on in Jesus' mind at this time, yet we can infer from the passage that Jesus went with the elders in order to fulfill the centurion's request and heal his servant. Jesus didn't try to "straighten him out" or clarify for the elders that he was no "errand boy" of the Jewish community. He didn't say a word. In this case his compassion exceeded even the inclination another person might have to "set the record straight" as to why he was accompanying the Jewish elders. But Jesus' policy, his message, his mode of living was to do good to people regardless of whether they were friends or foes, whether they could pay him back or not, whether or not they understood who he was. He went with them to heal.

Sometime before Jesus reached the centurion's home, the centurion realized his mistake. Maybe it dawned on him that Jesus wasn't under the authority of the Jewish leaders; perhaps someone told him the nature of Jesus' other work. In any case, the centurion became mortified and begged Jesus not to continue.

> When [Jesus] was not far from the house, the centurion sent friends to say to him, "Lord, do not trouble yourself, for I am not worthy to have you come under my roof; therefore I did not presume to come to you. But only speak the word, and let my servant be healed. For I also am a man set under authority, with soldiers under me; and I say to one, 'Go,' and he goes, and to another, 'Come,' and he comes, and to my slave, 'Do this,' and the slave does it" (Luke 7:6–8).

Scholars differ on exactly what the centurion meant, but it seems to me what he was saying is that since he was a man under authority, he *assumed* that Jesus was also. He at first acted like his usual self by asking the Jews to bring Jesus. But when he realized that Jesus acted on his own volition, the centurion was absolutely ashamed of himself. He had ordered someone to do something who was not in anyone's "chain of command." Yet Jesus commended the centurion with great excitement:

> When Jesus heard this he was amazed at him, and turning to the crowd that followed him, he said, "I tell you, not even in Israel have I found such faith" (Luke 7:9).

The centurion eventually came to the proper understanding of Jesus without Jesus saying a word. But the interesting point, from our perspective, is that Jesus showed compassion to the man, regardless of his lack of understanding.

Clarity of Mission

Jesus reached a level of clarity in his message where he was able to maintain a life focus. Achieving clarity of our values, of *our* "message," is of great importance. It provides a filter through which to view the world. Not every encounter and every conversation is of equal value to us. Because compassion was the central principle of Jesus' message, he was more interested in dealing with raw expressions of human need than with the academic speculation of the scribes. For example, on one occasion someone in the crowd shouted out, "Teacher, tell my brother to divide the family inheritance with me" (Luke 12:13). Jesus responded abruptly, "Friend, who set me to be a judge or arbitrator over you?" (verse 14) Then he directed the conversation to one of his favorite topics, the importance of hearing and doing and responding to Jesus' message *each day.* Clarity about our central message or values provides a sense that life has priorities for us.

But Jesus also established clarity on his *mission,* which is the second clue to being able to maintain a life focus. This clarity gradually dawned on Jesus as he tried to live his call faithfully. The purpose of this section is to understand how Jesus came to the belief that he needed to die in Jerusalem and that his death would provide life for many.

Let's return to the call of Jesus at his baptism and the uncertainty he faced as a result. He was the kingly Son and the lowly servant. He was the one who could ask and receive authority over the nations and, at the same time, he would not lift up his voice in the streets. How would Jesus "resolve" this tension? Our first indication occurs during Jesus' first sermon delivered to worshipers in Nazareth (Luke 4:16–30). He referred to Isaiah 61:1–2 and then said, "Today this scripture has been fulfilled in your hearing." The words from that passage in Isaiah bear repeating to see how Jesus first tried to "resolve" the issue of his mission:

> The Spirit of the Lord is upon me, because he has anointed me to bring good news to the poor. He has sent me to proclaim release to the captives and recovery of sight to the blind, to let the oppressed go free, to proclaim the year of the Lord's favor (Luke 4:18–19).

Jesus would preach good news and heal. But at this point he saw himself increasingly as a prophet, one who proclaims the Word of God. Perhaps he would model himself on the early biblical prophets Elijah and Elisha, who both proclaimed the message of God and were able to heal. He had not "abandoned" his self-understanding as King or as Servant; rather, he was postponing those roles to attend to the healing and proclaiming work of a prophet. As he set out on his mission, healing and speaking with authority, I don't believe Jesus could see the end of the journey; all he could do was be faithful to the light that he had.

Most of Jesus' early actions raised eyebrows. He healed people; he taught with authority and not as their scribes; he forgave sins. People were first amazed and gratified by the eruptive and electric presence of Jesus in their midst. But soon the grumbling started. Some people wondered why Jesus associated with tax collectors and sinners (Mark 2:16); some wanted to know why he and his disciples didn't fast when it was customary for religious leaders to do so (Mark 2:18); some were incensed that Jesus would heal on the Sabbath (Mark 3:1–6). Opposition began to form—especially in regard to the issue of healing on the Sabbath.

> The Pharisees went out and immediately conspired with the Herodians against him, how to destroy him (Mark 3:6).

Jesus must have known that opposition to him was developing. In the next chapter I will propose that Jesus' spiritual awareness was key to his ability to heal. He certainly had to know that his healing on the Sabbath would provoke an irreparable breach between him and the Jewish leaders. So why did he do it? If he knew it was going to cause extreme pain for the community and for himself, why not wait until the next day to do the healing? The healed person would be no worse off, and Jesus' relationship with the community would be preserved. Why didn't Jesus consider the cost of his rash action of Sabbath healing?

Most of us are taught that if you want to "get ahead" in life, you must pick your fights wisely and sparingly. When you are just starting out in a profession, it's preferable not to have any fights at all. It is better to smooth ruffled feathers than to insist on showing independence. The attitude most desired today is that of "team players." How can we sympathize with Jesus' act of defiance, his deliberate distancing himself from the leaders of his community? How can we understand the cost, the uncertainty that must have dogged him, the sense that he had burned all of his bridges behind him unless we too have chosen to alienate ourselves from people over an issue of principle? Who can fail to see that Jesus' healing on the Sabbath was, to him, one of integrity to his prophetic vocation, even though the religious leaders perceived it as an act of deliberate provocation?

Jesus spent that night in prayer, according to Luke (6:12). Most translations and scholars associate this all-night prayer session with Jesus' anticipation of choosing his disciples (6:13–16). Yet doesn't it also make sense to connect Jesus' all-night prayer vigil with his attempt to sort out all the issues involved in the irreparable breach with the religious community that he had precipitated that very day? He may have thought, *Should I confess that I have been hasty and rash? Try publicly to defend myself? Ignore the incident? How should I continue in relationship to the com-*

munity? Must I leave? Some of these questions no doubt filled Jesus' mind as he spent the entire night in prayer after the first Sabbath healing "incident."

But Jesus decided that he must continue his work of healing and teaching, even on the Sabbath. The die was cast, and he could not turn back now. His commitment intensified after a visit from the followers of John the Baptist and John's subsequent death. John's disciples came to Jesus, asking him if he was the one "who is to come" or whether they should look for another (Luke 7:20). Jesus responded in words taken right out of the Book of Isaiah:

> Go and tell John what you have seen and heard: the blind receive their sight, the lame walk, the lepers are cleansed, the deaf hear, the dead are raised, the poor have good news brought to them (Luke 7:22).

Jesus was saying that the prophetic work of healing and proclaiming would continue. Not much later, John was beheaded by Herod, whom he had offended. Jesus, as well as John, no doubt knew that the role of the prophet was to speak the truth, to stand up for principle and be willing to die for that truth. Yet perhaps John's death gave the matter a new reality for Jesus.

This new perspective, that he would die for his beliefs, was first verbalized when Jesus asked the disciples who they thought he really was (Luke 9:18–22). The disciples responded that people likened him to John the Baptist, Elijah or one of the prophets of long ago. So far, so good. But then Jesus asked for the disciples' opinion, to which Peter answered, "The Messiah of God" (Luke 9:20).

Bravo! The Messiah, in Jewish theology of Jesus' time, was perceived as a royal figure. When Peter confessed Jesus as Messiah, it meant that *both* Jesus' kingly and prophetic sides were coming out through his work. Jesus then wanted to take his disciples even deeper into his confidence, so he described to them the ultimate destiny of his death and resurrection:

The Son of Man must undergo great suffering, and be rejected by the elders, chief priests, and scribes, and be killed, and on the third day be raised (9:22).

But how did Jesus learn that his destiny would be to die in *Jerusalem* (verse 51) rather than at the hands of a crazed mob or a mugging on a dark country road? The confident belief that he would die in Jerusalem came, no doubt, through prayer. When Moses and Elijah appeared with Jesus at his transfiguration, they talked about Jesus' impending "departure, which he was about to accomplish at Jerusalem" (9:31). Jesus perhaps surmised by the nature of his opposition that he *probably* would die in Jerusalem, but he learned in prayer that his destiny was *definitely* to die in Jerusalem.

So, armed with this knowledge Jesus started off on his journey to Jerusalem.

When the days drew near for him to be taken up, he set his face to go to Jerusalem (Luke 9:51).

Now there is an urgency, a direction, a clear goal in mind.

Today, tomorrow, and the next day I must be on my way, because it is impossible for a prophet to be killed outside of Jerusalem. Jerusalem, Jerusalem, the city that kills the prophets and stones those who are sent to it! (Luke 13:33–34).

Jesus now knows where he is going. He is clear on his mission as well as his message. Fully sixty percent of the Gospel of Luke, containing Jesus' most memorable parables, follows Jesus' departure for Jerusalem. Once the message and the mission were clear, there was still time for many of his most moving teachings. Incredible depth results from clarity in message and method. Time, as it were, slows down so that the alert reader has a chance to catch every precious morsel from the lips of Jesus, the one who now speaks with a clear message and mission in mind.

Jesus and the Press of Time

Time confuses us. Some people say, "Life is long; take your time." Other people, or maybe even some of the same people, say, "Life is too short for that!" We say that it just seems "like yesterday" that some vivid event took place—when the event may actually be thirty years old. Events of the previous week may seem like they took places ages ago. At times the days fly by; other times they crawl. Augustine, the great father of the church who had something profound to say about nearly everything, said, "When you don't ask me what time is, I know, but if you inquire about what it is, I don't know."

How did Jesus deal with the limited time allotted to him? Did it hinder or help him in maintaining his focus? On one hand, Jesus must have felt a sense of constraint, an awareness of the clock ticking.

> I came to bring fire to the earth, and how I wish it were already kindled! I have a baptism with which to be baptized, and what stress I am under until it is completed (Luke 12:49–50).

Certainly, his mission weighed upon him. He would maintain a certain sense of incompleteness, of having lived only partially, until the final unfolding of his life's drama at Jerusalem.

Yet, on the other hand, Jesus lived in freedom with respect to time. A recurrent refrain in the early chapters of the Gospel of John is Jesus' statement, "My hour has not yet come" (John 2:4; 7:6). It is only before Jesus' final Passover that John says:

> Now before the festival of the Passover, Jesus knew that his hour had come to depart from this world and go to the Father (John 13:1).

His time was short, yet his life was relaxed, without hurry or rush, and more attuned to showing mercy than to watching the clock. His life was free, but destined; chosen, but constrained.

The paradox of freedom within constraint, or vice versa, is neatly expressed in Luke 13. Some Pharisees came to warn Jesus that Herod wanted to kill him. Rather than feeling fear or altering his course, Jesus responded:

> Go and tell that fox for me, "Listen, I am casting out demons and performing cures today and tomorrow, and on the third day I finish my work. Yet today, tomorrow, and the next day I must be on my way" (Luke 13:32–33).

The first part of the quotation emphasizes Jesus' freedom. In the face of Herod's threats, Jesus says he will finish his work. He *will not* be rushed by any human authority; he will go at the pace that fits his internal rhythms which are attuned to God's will. It is the extent of the work, rather than man-made pressure, that determines Jesus' attitude. That is the freedom of Jesus with respect to time.

Some people use "freedom" to mask indolence or lack of direction. Jesus did not do that. He used the phrase, "today, tomorrow and the next day" in the second part of the quotation to emphasize that he must be moving along. It was not a human or temporal force moving him toward his date with destiny in Jerusalem, but rather his sense of the call of God. Jesus' focused life kept him aware of the delicate balance between freedom and constraint. Time certainly pressed upon him, like the eager crowds yearning to touch even the hem of his garments. Yet as he inched his way to Jerusalem, he had ample time to deliver teachings and parables that still, 2000 years later, occupy our minds for a lifetime.

The secret of Jesus' mastery of time was his instinctive ability to trust God. In the words of Johann Sebastian Bach, "God's time is the very best time." On the cross, when Jesus uttered his last cry to God, he quoted words of trust from Psalm 31: "Father, into your hands I commend my spirit" (Luke 23:46, quoting Ps. 31:5). I like to suppose that, if one listened very closely, Jesus may have quoted the entire Psalm. If so, just a few verses later, he would have said, "I trust in you, O Lord. . . . My times are in your hand" (Ps. 31:14–15).

Jesus' death not only redeemed us from our sins, but re-deemed time from being meaningless. All time is God's time. Therefore, rejoice and shout for joy, since our times too, our times of confusion and blessing, are in the hands of a gracious God.

⌣•

Dear Jesus, I read and understand how focused you were. How your love was directed toward liberating people. How your words spoke to the hearts of people who needed your grace, healing and renewal. Your touch was directed towards those who suffered. Everything about you Lord Jesus was focused. Was it because you loved God and your neighbour? Was it because you knew intuitively what it meant to experience a deeper walk with God? You were focused in your love, you were focused in your grace, you were focused in your touch, and those liberated and freed and engaged people in new areas and in new hopes and possibilities. Lord my life is unfocused. I give a little attention to this, a little to that, and I find that I missed the mark at the end of the day. Jesus teach me to be focused on things that count. I think I know what does count: to be focused on the love of God, to be focused on prayer, and to be focused on scriptures. If I focus upon you when I choose those things, I have a center, I have a central core, and I have a foundation. Amen.

WARMING
THE
WORLD

PART
THREE

THE OUTER LIFE
OF JESUS

6

JESUS AND HEALING

The wounded surgeon plies the steel That questions the dis-
tempered part; Beneath the bleeding hands we feel The sharp
compassion of the healer's art.

—T. S. Eliot, *Four Quartets*

I saw afresh the depth of human physical and mental anguish
when I went on a short-term mission trip to Honduras in
1996. I accompanied a group of veterinarians, mostly from
Texas. The purpose of the trip was to immunize large and small
animals in Siguatepeque, a town of about 40,000 people, in
the central highlands. We also set up a medical clinic at the
local Episcopal church. My reason for going was to accompany my wife, observe the mission, be of help where needed
and help plan a similar trip in the future. Within one day of
arriving, however, I was conscripted by the American pedia-
trician, who knew no Spanish, to translate as she tried to understand and diagnose the people who came to her at the medical clinic. At first I was hesitant to do this; my Spanish was
quite rusty, and I didn't relish trying to translate the emotion-
laden phrases that poured from the lips of distraught people.
Nevertheless, I tried my best and managed to communicate
the essence of most of the ailments to the doctor.

One day, just as we were about to close the clinic, a woman
brought in a man who appeared to be blind. He was old and
grizzled, with small features and hunched shoulders that com-

municated silently the message, "I wish I could just disappear." He had a dirty patch over one eye that probably had not been changed in months. The doctor removed the patch gingerly. We both winced as a large puffy mass of flesh seemed to fall right out of his eye and dangle against his cheek, held in place by some flimsy roots of flesh. I thought it was his eye, held in place by the patch, but the doctor told me to explain that he had a tumor.

As I talked to the woman and the old man, I learned that the tumor had been growing for about ten years. It was so painful that the only relief the old man could get was to keep both eyes closed. On one occasion he had tried to go by bus to Tegucigalpa, the capital, to get treatment. But he had become disoriented and had fallen, so he dragged himself back to the bus station for the two-hour return ride to Siguatepeque. He then pulled up his pant leg to show us a series of deep bruises on his shins, the result of his repeatedly walking into things and falling. The doctor was not equipped for surgery, so all she could do was rebandage the man's eye.

The next morning, however, as our group gathered in a prayer circle before starting work for the day, the doctor described the man's problem. She mentioned that if we could come up with $100, he could go to a private doctor and have the tumor removed. Silently, after her announcement, people from our circle took money to the doctor. She began to cry, because what she hoped would be $100 soon became $350. He would have the operation. Yet our hope in 1996 was tempered in 1997 when we learned, during our May trip, that the man had recently died.

Another man came with two dogs for immunization. He spoke some English and appeared to be quite outgoing. "I love America as a second country, though I have never been there," he said. After his dogs were immunized, he stood at attention in the middle of the field and, at the top of his lungs, sang the first stanza of the "Star-Spangled Banner."

Later he joined some of us at the large animal clinic. We asked him to sing the Honduran national anthem, and he readily complied. Then he told us he was a manic-depressive and could not get treatment in Honduras. When he was subject to one of his depressive episodes, people said that he had a "demon" and refused to deal with him. He was unable to work because of the unpredictability of his moods. He lived with his mother, who had a modest pension, and together they eked out a meager existence.

What struck me about the man during our conversation was his deep intelligence and knowledge of the world. He told me how various states in the United States were considering legislation to extend medical benefits to people who suffered from his condition. He seemed to be aware of the struggles for recognition the mental health profession has faced in the twentieth century. Then, abruptly, he ended our conversation and headed home, singing vigorously. Obviously, he was in a manic phase.

As I returned from Honduras, I thought a lot about disease and healing. Mental and physical distress were much a part of Jesus' world, and they remain with us today. Despite huge advances in medical knowledge, we continue to be plagued by a bewildering array of diseases. New illnesses are "discovered" as others are eradicated. Mental and physical disease are so debilitating, so enervating. Disease affects not only the sufferer but also the network of people who are touched by his or her life. Disease takes a person out of the "loop" of conversation and activity which are valued elements of "normal" living. The ravages of disease reduce us to shadows of our healthy state.

Jesus' Healing Ministry and Spiritual Awareness

I believe the key to Jesus' ability to heal rested in his spiritual perception, his ability to "see into" people, to discern and diagnose their "spiritual maladies," to touch their "pressure points" in order to relieve their distresses. I don't think Jesus' healing ability depended on some so-called divine "power-pack" that he could "switch on" for those he wanted to heal. His healing capability grew out of his rich humanity, his ability to discern in a moment the most intimate longings and needs of the human heart. It was a skill he developed through years of patient listening to God in prayer, in studying the Scriptures, and in his attempt to be faithful to his call.

Healing seemed to require a partnership of sorts. Jesus needed not only his own spiritual awareness, but also the willingness and spiritual capacity of those he healed. This is the only way to understand Mark 6:1–5, a problem passage for scholars who look at Jesus' healing in the "power-pack" mode. Jesus had just returned home to speak at the synagogue. People's reaction was a mixture of unbelief and offense:

> "Where did this man get all this? What is this wisdom that has been given to him? What deeds of power are being done by his hands! Is not this the carpenter, the son of Mary and brother of James and Joses and Judas and Simon, and are not his sisters here with us?" And they took offense at him (verses 2–3).

Their reaction was something to the effect of: "You can't be all that great, kid, because we know who you are. We know your family. We know you are no different than one of us. Don't try to be some kind of high and mighty teacher. Realize who you are!"

The result of this treatment in his hometown is recorded in Mark 6:5:

> And he could do no deed of power there, except that he laid his hands on a few sick people and cured them.

Jesus' healing power is hindered by unbelief. It is almost as if his power is perceived as some kind energy flow that will not have its desired effect unless the recipient completes the connection. In his hometown, Jesus could not do his customary wonders.

So if Jesus' healing power was not some kind of magical force, how can we best describe it? What is this "spiritual awareness" of which we have been referring? Three points will help to clarify this claim. Jesus' healing power consisted, first, in his ability to *know the human heart*. Jesus could, as it were, look into a person's soul and discern not simply the condition of the heart but also his or her deepest aspirations and yearnings.

The first few chapters of John show Jesus at his discerning best. The Gospel of John has been known, since the second century, as the "spiritual Gospel," because it provides the best picture of Jesus' inner life.

We first see Jesus' spiritual discernment in the call of Simon Peter to discipleship. Andrew, Simon Peter's brother, met Jesus first and then told Simon, "We have found the Messiah" (John 1:41). Andrew took Simon to Jesus, and Jesus said, "You are Simon son of John. You are to be called Cephas, (which is translated Peter)" (John 1:42).

The name Peter means "rock" or "stone." Though one could explain this name change in a number of ways, the most convincing explanation is that Jesus immediately perceived something about the character of Simon that revealed rock-like stability. By giving a name, Jesus was inspiring a person. Jesus selected a name that would draw out the best in Peter, that would encourage him when he failed, that would help him recognize what he could yet become.

A similar instance occurs again in John 1, this time with Nathanael.

> Philip found Nathanael and said to him, "We have found him about whom Moses in the law and also the prophets wrote, Jesus son of Joseph from Nazareth" (John 1:45).

Nathanael expressed skepticism when Philip invited him to come and meet Jesus. But when Jesus saw Nathanael, Jesus said, "Here is truly an Israelite in whom there is no deceit!" (John 1:47)

Nathanael wanted to know how Jesus could know anything about him, since they had never met. Jesus responded, "I saw you under the fig tree before Philip called you" (John 1:48).

Nathanael then confessed his faith: "Rabbi, you are the Son of God! You are the King of Israel!" (John 1:49)

What is powerful about this encounter is that Jesus had perceived, through observing Nathanael, that he was a person of integrity who aspired to wholeness in his conduct. Jesus was a healer because he could perceive the deepest longings in people's hearts and inspire them to live up to their best inclinations.

Second, Jesus also knew how to *ask the crucial question* that released a flood of emotions or long pent-up feelings. This is most evident in the healing of the lame man at the pool of Beth-zatha (John 5). Jesus saw the man at the pool's edge, and immediately knew he had been there a long time (John 5:6). Perhaps Jesus saw his torn clothing, his dirty appearance, his makeshift shelter. In addition, Jesus knew that being near a healing pool a long time without being healed would make the man wonder if he ever would become better. So, Jesus asked him a crucial question: "Do you want to be made well?" (John 5:6)

Some people in this situation would be depressed and resigned to never being first in the water to be healed. The only joy in their life would be the perverse irony of *knowing* that they would never be healed. *Never.*

Jesus' question shows that he not only wants to heal people, but also wants to appeal to our own will and self-knowledge as a means of bringing about our healing.

A third factor of Jesus' healing ability was that he knew how to *extend true sympathy* to the distressed. He was a spiritual physician who was touched by the pain of people. A clear example of this is the story of the curing of a deaf man. It shows Jesus' ability to preserve the dignity of the sufferer as he brought about the person's health.

> Then he returned from the region of Tyre, and went by way of Sidon towards the Sea of Galilee, in the region of the Decapolis. They brought to him a deaf man who had an impediment in his speech; and they begged him to lay his hand on him. He took him aside in private, away from the crowd, and put his fingers into his ears, and he spat and touched his tongue. Then looking up to heaven, he sighed and said to him, "Eph-

phatha," that is, "Be opened." And immediately his ears were opened, his tongue was released, and he spoke plainly (Mark 7:31–35).

This story is a wonderfully rich one. It reveals at least four things about Jesus and his healing. The first thing we learn is that Jesus, by taking the deaf man aside, wanted to preserve a singular intimacy with the man. People weren't healed en masse; each person was treated as a worthwhile individual. Jesus took the deaf man away from the noise of the crowd, quietly perceived his need, and healed him.

Second, Jesus used the common act of touching and the common element of spittle as symbols of healing. It is not that the actions or the spittle *produced* the healing; they were Jesus' way of illustrating that healing can take place through basic human elements and actions. Jesus demonstrated that clay can heal clay and that even though people shall return to dust, they are worthy of the wholeness that healing can bring. Jesus' healing of the deaf man ennobled forever the human actions of sympathetic touching and sharing to bring about healing.

Third, the word translated "he sighed" in verse 34 is better rendered, "he groaned." This suggests that Jesus' reaction to the deaf man's condition was not one of pity or regret, but of deep and aching anguish. It is similar to the word Paul used in Romans 8:22: "We know that the whole creation has been groaning in labor pains until now."

Jesus' groaning is the emotion of a man who realizes how tangled the realities of life have become; how dominant the powers of illness and evil appear to be; how seemingly hopeless life can become. It is a groan that signifies all the heartache of the world and all the yearnings for wholeness and life.

Finally, Jesus' words to the man, "Be opened," are important. Jesus spoke to the *person* and not to his tongue, to the *man* and not to his ears. The man needed to be opened, and his hearing would thereby be restored. Jesus' act of healing is an act of restoring and opening the *whole person*. The man's tongue was released, but more importantly, his soul was opened.

The healing ministry of Jesus shows us that the most important spiritual need in the world is awareness—of the spiritual realities of any situation and the breadth of spiritual vision needed to deal with the nature of the world wherever you are. By demonstrating his deep knowledge of people and a sincere sympathy for them, Jesus both inspires us and humbles us to be healers in our own day.

Healing of the Mind—The Gerasene Demoniac

In Psalm 65, the psalmist praises God who visits and waters the earth, who provides good things for His people. Verse 7 says:

> You silence the roaring of the seas,
> the roaring of their waves,
> the tumult of the peoples.

At one point in his ministry, Jesus finished stilling the roaring of the sea (Mark 4:35–41) and almost immediately began to deal with the tumult of the people. In this instance, the problem was the swirling mental tumult of a man possessed by a legion of demons (Mark 5:1–20). The man was not in his right mind. He not only experienced the *distortion* of himself as created in the image of God, but also the *near-destruction* of that image. That Jesus would enter his life, perceive the depth of his need, and expel the demons that enslaved him displays Jesus' knowledge of the human heart and depth of sympathy with our condition. The account also shows the skill of the Gospel writer in describing the hopelessness and severity of mental distress. It is a story fraught with human pathos.

The passage begins with the description of the man's *condition:*

> They came to the other side of the sea, to the country of the Gerasenes. And when he had stepped out of the boat, immediately a man out of the tombs with an unclean spirit met him. He lived among the tombs; and no one could restrain him any

more, even with a chain; for he had often been restrained with shackles and chains, but the chains he wrenched apart, and the shackles he broke in pieces; and no one had the strength to subdue him. Night and day among the tombs and on the mountains he was always howling and bruising himself with stones (Mark 5:1–5).

Since Jesus was in an unclean (non-Jewish) land, it was not unusual for him to be confronted by a man with an unclean spirit. The Greek text suggests many things about the situation. One significant clue is the word "immediately" in verse 2. Except for a few instances, this word is used in reference to Jesus throughout the Gospel of Mark. It stresses the urgency and rapid pace of his ministry. In this exception, however, it is used to describe the action of the possessed man. It is a subtle hint that a huge confrontation is brewing.

Then there is a long, pathetic description of the man's condition. The text says three times that he lived among the tombs. An attentive reader should note the power of death that surrounds him.

A third significant factor is his superhuman strength. The Greek text is particularly forceful in stressing that no one, at any time, could subdue or bind him with any chain. The man could free himself from chains, but not from the demonic forces within him. He could break his bonds, but not unravel the labyrinthine tangle of his ravaged mind. The Talmud, a Jewish holy book from antiquity, mentions four conditions of madness: walking about at night, spending the night on a grave, tearing one's clothes and destroying what one has been given. The man in this passage fits the definition to a T.

But when we probe deeper, we see that he was not simply possessed by a demonic force. He also was made in the image of God, and his true self was struggling for release. Two questions will help bring this matter into focus: (1) Why did he live among the tombs? and (2) What does it mean that he cried out and cut himself with stones?

One possible reason for his living among the tombs is that he was an outcast from society. They couldn't handle him; they didn't want him; they had, as it were, consigned him to death. Such is the scholarly consensus. But I also detect in his living among tombs a glimpse of his sanity, a glimmer of his desire to be made well. He was living among tombs because at least *there* he found people who wouldn't reject him; at least *there* he could possibly read the names of the departed and yearn for a time when the condition of his mind would not be so tumultuous. It was an expression of his deep human longing for fellowship, for inclusion in the life of a community. My interpretation makes the man truly tormented because he *knew* in the recesses of his being that he needed the human contact which was being denied him.

Why did he cut himself with stones? Again, the scholarly consensus is that this action was evidence either of his attempts to commit suicide or to worship the forces of darkness. His behavior is compared to the action of the priests of Baal who "cut themselves" to get their God's attention (1 Kings 18:28). This interpretation assumes the man was acting, maybe even being forced to act, to serve demonic forces.

I see the cutting of his flesh, rather, as a deliberate and reasonable attempt to release the spirits that haunted him. He knew he was not well and that the source of his malady was some powerful force within him. If only he could "let it out," maybe, just maybe there was a chance he could be made well. I see the man as a distraught human instead of a brainwashed automaton, a man convulsed by movements he couldn't understand but which he fought vainly to control. He was losing the battle with his mind.

In this connection it is interesting to consider David Halberstam's treatment of the suicide of Philip Graham, former publisher of the *Washington Post*, as described in *The Powers That Be*. One of the most brilliant men of his generation, Graham was also afflicted by a form of manic-depression that even the most advanced medication and treatment couldn't control. One day Graham committed suicide. Most people thought the evil force of his depression had so overwhelmed him that he was literally driven to suicide. Others contended, and Halberstam seems to agree, that Graham's suicide was a rational choice, deliberately enacted because he realized he just wasn't getting any better and had no real hope that he would. It was Graham's attempt, in a curious sort of way, to preserve the tattered shreds of his battered humanity. Perhaps the demon-possessed Gerasene man was trying to do something similar, hoping he would someday be healed through his cutting. If so, it adds to the pathos of the man's condition.

We next see the man's *confusion* (Mark 5:6–10). The text says:

> When he saw Jesus from a distance, he ran and bowed down before him; and he shouted at the top of his voice, "What have you to do with me, Jesus, Son of the Most High God? I adjure you by God, do not torment me." For he had said to him, "Come out of the man, you unclean spirit!" Then Jesus asked him, "What is your name?" He replied, "My name is Legion; for we are many." He begged him earnestly not to send them out of the country.

When we look at the man's reaction to Jesus, he is torn. Confused. Riven. Split. He runs to Jesus, but wants Jesus to go away. He worships him, but begs not to be tormented. He is one, but there are many demons within him. The presence of Jesus, combined with the man's depth of spiritual perception, brought these almost intolerable inner conflicts to a head. Confusion reigned in his mind. The oppressiveness of his condition was made worse because he could not come to clarity about anything. His mind was tumbling further and further out of control. William Styron, in his moving autobiographical memoir, *Darkness Visible,* tells of the deep sense of terror, loneliness and confusion that hounded him during his depressive incidents. It was oppression beyond words, a fear that enveloped him like the darkness of the night.

Jesus spoke first and asked the demon to identify himself. It is said that in the name of the thing is the power of the thing, so perhaps this was a way to try to control these ravaging spirits. The man (or demon) responded that his name was, "Legion, for we are many." Numerous spirits were vying for control in the man.

Maybe the possessed man had seen the Roman Legion, the fiercest fighting force known to humanity at this time in history. They trained not far away on the treeless plains of the Decapolis. Had he looked up from the barren tombs and seen the well-disciplined columns of proud soldiers going through their exercises? A legion was the strongest fighting force imaginable and it was that kind of grip the demonic forces had on the man's life. They simply could not be mastered.

People today may be in a similar grip of forces beyond their control. I have seen the grip of alcoholism that convinces some people to choose the bottle over their families and jobs. I have seen the iron grasp of lust, greed and grief and anger—especially anger. It is almost as if victims of these forces are in the power of a multi-headed demon called "Legion."

Yet after the demon-possessed man's confusion, there was a *confrontation* that led to the man's *consolation*.

> Now there on the hillside a great herd of swine was feeding; and the unclean spirits begged him, "Send us into the swine; let us enter them." So he gave them permission. And the unclean spirits came out and entered the swine; and the herd, numbering about two thousand, rushed down the steep bank into the sea, and were drowned in the sea (Mark 5:11–13).

A deal was struck between Jesus and Legion. The demonic force may have been strong, but it was no match for Jesus. He sent the Legion into a group of pigs feeding nearby. There has been a lot of discussion about Jesus' reason for permitting the destruction of so much life in this instance, but I see it as an illustration of the principle set forth in his Sermon on the Mount:

> Look at the birds of the air; they neither sow nor reap nor gather into barns, and yet your heavenly Father feeds them. Are you not of more value than they? (Matt. 6:26)

The man, even in his distraught, deformed and nearly destroyed condition was of so much more value than the pigs that Jesus' action was warranted. The value of two thousand pigs pales in comparison to the value of one human—even a troubled outcast like this man. So the unclean spirits went into the unclean swine in the unclean country, causing the pigs to rush down the hill and drown. Imagine the dramatic silence that resulted.

Finally, the passage concludes with the man's *comfort:*

> The swineherds ran off and told it in the city and in the country. Then the people came to see what it was that had happened. They came to Jesus and saw the demoniac sitting there, clothed and in his right mind, the very man who had had the legion; and they were afraid. Those who had seen what had happened to the demoniac and to the swine reported it. Then they began to beg Jesus to leave their neighborhood. As he was getting into the boat, the man who had been possessed by demons begged him that he might be with him. But Jesus refused, and said to him, "Go home to your friends, and tell them how much the Lord has done for you, and what mercy he has shown you." And he went away and began to proclaim in the Decapolis how much Jesus had done for him; and everyone was amazed (Mark 5:14–20).

The people came to see what had happened. What they saw must have taken their breath away. They saw a man, formerly out of control, now in his right mind. He was sitting instead of running around; clothed and not naked; quiet and not shrieking. So why were they afraid? Perhaps this was only a lull before the real storm of the man's emotional distress? More likely they realized they had witnessed the result of the confrontation between the very powers of evil and good on that fateful day. While calming one person's life, Jesus' presence threatened to disrupt everyone else's. Jesus had brought a person from the fringes of society right into the heart of his own saving work. If he could do that, what was to prevent him from removing those at the center of society to the fringes? Jesus' healing, though dramatic and moving, was too much to comprehend. That is why they chose to beg Jesus to leave the country.

Jesus healed the afflicted man by seeing deeply into his heart and touching the profound springs of the man's longing to be well. Oh, Lord, heal our ravaged and confused minds today.

The Healing of the Body—The Woman with a Flow of Blood

I have been sick while writing this chapter. When my fever, cough, aches, and sleeplessness first came on me several days ago, I thought I should stop writing until I had recovered. Why put additional stress on the body and mind when the task of writing is already difficult? But I decided to press ahead, feeling that if I wrote about Jesus and healing when I was not well, I might discover some insights about sickness and healing not available to me in a healthy state.

I think the most important thing I have learned is how the weakness of being sick can contribute to a general feeling of hopelessness and loss of control. I realized in my sickness, for example, that I was unable to control whether or not I slept at night. I remember the first night of my feverish condition. I watched the local news before retiring, noting that the weather forecast for the next day ranged from 97 degrees in Wichita to 107 degrees in Ponca City, Oklahoma. As I dropped into a fitful sleep, I began to dream.

I dreamed I was in my convertible, speeding toward Ponca City with the top down. I arrived there with the sun beating down on me and the temperature reading 107 degrees. I woke up sweating, coughing, and utterly drained. By morning my fever had subsided, but it began to return by midday. I no longer felt able to fix meals for the children, to keep the house clean, even to read. I began to see myself languishing, severed from the cycle of life with no strength to return to it. One evening I tried to "force" the sickness from my body by calling friends and speaking on the phone for three hours. I tried to defy the illness—to deny that it had any control over me. But after I hung up, the fever returned with a virulence I had not previously felt. It was as if the fever was saying to me, "I am in charge of your life now! Don't forget it!"

In my fever and weakness I read about the woman with a hemorrhage of blood. For the first time, I felt that I understood some of her fears and weakness. Her story is told in the first three Gospels, but the account in Mark is the richest:

> Now there was a woman who had been suffering from hemorrhages for twelve years. She had endured much under many physicians, and had spent all that she had; and she was no better, but rather grew worse. She had heard about Jesus, and came up behind him in the crowd and touched his cloak, for she said, "If I but touch his clothes, I will be made well." Immediately her hemorrhage stopped; and she felt in her body that she was healed of her disease. Immediately aware that power had gone forth from him, Jesus turned about in the crowd and said, "Who touched my clothes?" And his disciples said to him, "You see the crowd pressing in on you; how can you say, 'Who touched me?'" He looked all around to see who had done it. But the woman, knowing what had happened to her, came in fear and trembling, fell down before him, and told him the whole truth. He said to her, "Daughter, your faith has made you well; go in peace, and be healed of your disease" (Mark 5:25–34).

This story is inserted into another healing story, the resurrection of Jairus' twelve-year-old daughter. Jesus had been approached by Jairus, a leader of the synagogue, who desperately sought help for his dying daughter. There was real urgency and need in Jairus' appeal. On the way to see Jairus' daughter, Jesus had the encounter related above. It illustrates a major lesson of life, that while we are on the way to one place, something unexpected may happen which changes our lives—or someone else's.

The first thing to note in the passage is the *debility* of the woman. The word *hemorrhage* refers to a "flow of blood" she had suffered with for twelve years. Perhaps only a woman could comprehend the feeling of weakness, wanness, and enervation this would bring about. In addition to the weakness, the flow of blood made her religiously unclean. She would be required to keep her distance from crowds and religious people, lest the taint of her uncleanness be spread to them. How would it feel to know that each day of your life your blood is still flowing out of you and that you'll never regain your strength until it stops? Perhaps an analogy from today would be those who suffer from chronic fatigue syndrome. Just the task of getting out of bed seems to take all one's energy allotment for the day.

The woman's weakness led to her acts of *desperation*. Desperation frequently precedes healing in the Gospel accounts. Desperation results from an awareness of one's own need combined with the inability to do anything about fulfilling it. In this instance the woman had gone to various physicians for treatment and spent all her money, yet grew steadily worse. The best treatment she could afford only hastened her decline. Nothing could remedy her situation. When a disease of this magnitude afflicts you (the Greek word for *disease* in this passage is more accurately translated "scourge" or "whipping"), it becomes the most pressing and all-consuming issue of life. You become "intoxicated" by your illness, to use a phrase by Anatole Broyard. All of life is affected by it. It becomes your lord and master, demanding ever more of your allegiance.

I have noticed the way disease works in people, especially those gradually succumbing to old age. A friend of mine in his early 80's was, until about a year ago, a delightful conversationalist—witty, informed, thoughtful, full of stories and reminiscences. Now the aches and pains of his body require him to go to the doctor nearly every week. When I see him he is much more pensive and reserved. Sometimes all he can talk about is the doctor's report. His illness is starting to demand more and more of his attention. In some ways, I feel I am losing my friend because the illnesses of age are coming between him and me. Soon his wife may even take second place to them.

But the woman in the Mark account had something else that drove her to seek out Jesus—*determination*. She had heard reports about him and believed he could make her well. Her desperation had not strangled her hope. Why is it that some people become resigned to their condition and succumb to despair, while others still maintain the power of hope? How can some people see obstacles not as stumbling blocks, but as stepping stones? I believe that in the course of life we are all subject to various kinds of testing in order to determine the strength of our faith and character. Sickness is one of the most unforgiving and unrelenting forms of testing. Will it be the occasion to lose hope or to build character and the broad human virtue of sympathetic understanding?

Along with her determination was the willingness to *take a risk* to be made well. She probably should not even have been among the crowd, but she was there. She showed the kind of faith that the friends of the paralytic showed, who took the roof off a house so they could lower their afflicted friend right into the lap of Jesus (Mark 2:1–5). Perhaps she was thinking that since Jesus healed people on the Sabbath, he might also challenge the law in this instance by confronting an unclean woman. She really had nothing to lose.

Then, when she touched Jesus' garment, it was as if time stopped. Her flow of blood stopped. Jesus stopped and turned. The crowd stopped. Her flow of blood was replaced by a flow of gratitude. Did the woman feel the healing like a jolt of electricity through her, as if she had just been energized by an outside force, or was it more like something leaving her, like a fever that breaks and leaves us in our right mind? Was something added, or taken away? In my own case, I remember the feverish night I was driving to Ponca City in my dreams. After I awoke, cleaned myself up and lay back down to sleep, a tremendous feeling of peace surged through me. The fever left. Instead of resuming the drive to Ponca City, I could hear the words of the psalmist, "he gives sleep to his beloved" (Ps. 127:2). I then slept peacefully for three hours.

But there was an awkward moment when Jesus stopped and asked who had touched him. As usual, the disciples tried to paper over Jesus' real concerns with reasonable, but shallow and irrelevant comments. Yet Jesus would not be deterred. Jesus knew and the woman seemed to know, that Jesus was on a healing vigil and not on parade. Jesus was interested in touching lives and not in signing autographs. Spiritual discerners recognize each other, and even though the crowd thronged around, the woman and Jesus knew that they were really the only two actors in this scene. Jesus may be compared to a master teacher who, by posing one question, can discern in a class of 100 students the five or six who really comprehend the subject matter.

The final scene of the story was the woman's coming forward, in fear and trembling, to admit that indeed she had touched his garment. Why in fear and trembling? How could she, who showed so much determination and hope only a few verses before, now be subject to these emotions? Because people who have been at the mercy of ravaging forces know that they are vulnerable people. Even though the woman might not have expected her torment to continue, she would understand if it did. She had been a victim for twelve years—to the disease and to the doctors. Why should her victimization stop now? She who had been clobbered by life may just be clobbered again.

But what did she do? In a moment of remarkable depth and daring, she "told [Jesus] the whole truth" (Mark 5:33). Oh to have been there and to have heard her! What would her statement have consisted of? Certainly it would contain a litany of her disease and failed attempts at effective treatment. By now she could recite this story as well as a preschool teacher telling nursery rhymes.

But she might also have included other items: how she had violated the law in being there, how she had put all her hope in Jesus, how she had *known* that if she touched his garment she would be made well. She realized she had nothing to hide, so she told Jesus the truth. Here was another Israelite in whom there was no deceit! In telling the whole truth, it must have been evident to Jesus and the disciples that what healed the woman was not the grasp of her hand, but the grasp of her faith. She was well, and commended and could go in peace.

There was life *after* disease, after that debilitating, enervating, draining flow of blood. Thanks be to God!

On a personal note, my temperature has returned to normal. I still have a cough and plan to take it easy for a few days, but I feel I have been coaxed back to health by the stories of the Gerasene demoniac and the woman with the flow of blood. I have seen afresh, in the Scriptures and in life, how illness weakens me, saps my strength, and even takes away my love of life. I have seen how illness, mental or physical, almost always has familial or social consequences. I have seen that it impedes the flow of life and, like Legion, takes over and demands to be served. But I have also seen Jesus, who seeks out people in their weaknesses, and wants to free us from the debilities of body and spirit. I place my hand on the folds of his garments and say, "May my sickness be with me no longer." I tell him the entire truth about my condition. And, to my joy, he is able to put me again in my right mind, clothed and seated and quiet, ready to listen to him.

~ •

Dear Jesus, I am so confused about healing. I see faith healers on the television proclaiming your power, and yet I see people in the hospital dying. I see people today grappling with illness and I pass them and I want to heal them or see them healed in your name. And yet Lord, I read the newspaper and I see where meditation and prayer aids those who are dying of cancer or some other illness. Lord Jesus I talk with people who are recovering from drugs, who have marital difficulties, and they seek healing. Jesus, you heal those who are in need. You touch those who are in pain. Your grace liberated and freed them, whether they were freed physically from a tumour, cancer, a cold or pneumonia, or emotionally from the demons that seem to clamour for attention. You are the healer, Jesus, you are the healer. You quietly go about touching those who need your grace and touching those who need your love. You bring healing power to those who cry out to you. And so Jesus, I see you as a healer. I see you as one touching those who are ill, touching those who are sad and downtrodden. You are still the healer. Heal our souls. Heal our minds. Heal our spirits. Amen.

7

JESUS AND SOCIAL JUSTICE

No place of grace for those who avoid the face No time to
rejoice for those who walk among noise and deny the voice

—T. S. Eliot, *Ash Wednesday*

One of the most memorable modern statements of the philosophy of Christian social justice and political involvement is Martin Luther King, Jr.'s, "Letter from Birmingham
City Jail." Written on April 16, 1963, while King was serving
time for having led an illegal protest march in that city, King's
letter answers charges brought against him and lays out his philosophy of "direct action." Usually King did not defend his
work or try to justify his action but in this instance he had been
stung by the criticism of eight prominent liberal white ministers in Birmingham who said his march had been ill-timed and
counterproductive.

In fifteen pages of concise reasoning, King made his case.
He had been criticized for being an outsider and bringing in
agitators to lead the march. King responded eloquently, "I am
cognizant of the interrelatedness of all communities and states."
Like the Apostle Paul, who heard the Macedonian call for aid
and responded to it, King was trying to be faithful to the call
of beleaguered brethren in Birmingham. King's position as
president of the Southern Christian Leadership Conference,
which had offices in Birmingham as well as eighty-four other
southern cities, made him sympathetic to the invitation of the
local chapter.

Then he laid out the four-fold nature of his work. First was the collection of facts to determine whether injustices existed; second was negotiation with the powers of the city for amelioration of the situation; third was a process of self-purification; fourth was non-violent direct action. On arriving in Birmingham, King and his associates surveyed the racial situation and met with merchants to see if offensive racial signs could be removed. They even put off their demonstration for months until the mayoral election was over, so that no accusation of partisan political activity could be lodged against them. But then, after no response was given to their demands, King and his followers engaged in "self-purification" and "direct action." Self-purification is the process of examining personal motives to determine if one is "fit" or "ready" for the demonstration and the possible consequences of it. Direct action consists of boycotts, marches, sit-ins, etc.

Why use such dramatic forms of action? Why not do something less confrontative and embarrassing? King knew that negotiation is always an important step, yet he discovered "through painful experience that freedom is never voluntarily given by the oppressor: it must be demanded by the oppressed." The goal of nonviolent direct action is to "create such a crisis and establish such creative tension that a community that has constantly refused to negotiate is forced to confront the issue." It was his experience that no progress in the area of civil rights has been made without pressure from the devotees of civil rights. Citing theologian Reinhold Niebuhr, King maintained that groups are more immoral than individuals. Therefore, in order to change the policy of a group, one sometimes has to resort to more extreme measures than one would use in the case of an individual.

Many criticisms were leveled at King. First, he had pursued his protest at an inopportune time; second, he broke laws by protesting; and third, his method of protest was too extreme. King responded to each of these charges.

To the accusation that his protest was untimely, King asked whether *any* time is really the right time for protest. There was no reason to believe that time alone would "heal this wound" or that, without intervention, segregation would eventually disappear and be replaced by full integration. King found it ironic that some people are willing, in a paternalistic fashion, to set the timetable for another's freedom. King's view of history was that there has been no necessity or inevitability to the black person's gaining his or her rights. They need to be contested, fought for, striven after. He wrote:

> We merely bring to the surface the hidden tension that is already alive. We bring it out in the open where it can be seen and dealt with. Like a boil that can never be cured as long as it is covered up but must be opened with all its pus-flowing ugliness to the natural medicines of air and light, injustice must likewise be exposed, with all of the tension its exposing creates . . . (*A Testament of Hope: The Essential Writings of Martin Luther King, Jr.,* p. 295).

To the charge that he had broken the law by protesting without the necessary permit, King argued that the goal of the Christian life is not to uphold all laws, but to obey just laws while seeking to change unjust ones. Drawing upon Augustine, Aquinas and centuries of Christian social teaching, King stated clearly, "An unjust law is no law at all." Therefore, if a person is convinced that laws of segregation are unjust, they are not to be obeyed, and protest is a legitimate method of questioning them. Hitler acted under the cloak of legality for years, yet there would be few people who would have condemned a protest to his unjust policies.

Finally, to the charge that his action was too extreme, King answered in two ways. On the one hand, he saw himself as a moderate, standing between two opposing forces in the black community. This perspective would be confirmed within two or three years, as the much more militant Black Panther Party and the Nation of Islam emerged. Yet, King also said, "I gradually gained a bit of satisfaction from being considered an extremist." Wasn't Jesus, too, an extremist when he taught us to love our enemies? Wasn't Paul an extremist for Christ? Wasn't

Martin Luther an extremist against the forces of medieval Catholicism when he said, "Here I stand; I can do no other. God help me"?

King wanted to show that the demands of Christian discipleship lead naturally to political involvement and social action. He lamented that so many ministers told him social issues were of no concern to the Gospel. Many of the white churches sat on the sidelines mouthing "pious irrelevancies and sanctimonious trivialities." He realized the church is in danger of "standing as a taillight behind other community agencies rather than a headlight leading men to higher levels of justice."

A More Recent Story of Social Justice

I was led to consider King's "Letter" afresh due to an experience I had in 1996 with political involvement in an issue of racial justice. The following story will show how wrenching it can be for a community to face issues of racial injustice. In my experience, as with Martin Luther King, the "messengers" are arrested or discredited, the issue is ignored as long as possible, and those accused maintain a tone of wounded moral indignation and religious righteousness.

In January 1996, while teaching at a small Christian College in the Midwest, I received word that Troy, one of my African-American advisees, had been cut from the basketball team. I wrote him a note, asking if he would like to talk to me about it. A few days later Troy appeared in my office. He is a bright, quiet, responsible, powerfully built young man who was known around campus as an approachable and personable Christian man. I told him I had heard he was upset over being cut from the team, and that I would be willing to help him in any way I could. I would also gladly bow out if he didn't want to talk about the issue.

Troy began to tell his story. For three years he had been the only African-American on the men's varsity basketball team. He knew the coach was never warm toward him, but he was willing to accept that as just an issue of personal chemistry—you can't be best friends with everybody. But at the beginning of his senior year, the coach took him and the only other minority player (a young Hispanic man) aside, and told them he didn't think there would be uniforms for them this year. Other, younger players needed to get some experience, and he couldn't assure them they would get a chance to play.

The other player was so distraught that he quit the team right away and kept the issue very quiet. But Troy refused to quit. He had worked for three years to play, and he was not going to go without a more substantial reason. The coach permitted Troy to stay, but rarely allowed him to play. Even in a humiliating forty point loss, Troy only got to play the last few seconds. The coach told him it just wasn't working out and proceeded to cut him. A trainer overheard the conversation, confirming that the coach had indeed cut Troy.

In December, Troy and three other players went to the Interim President of the College with an oral presentation of their complaints. The President assured them their concerns would be investigated.

When Troy came to see me near the end of January, the President had not gotten back to the players. I told Troy that my experience in life in general and at this college in particular was that potentially embarrassing issues are ignored as long as possible to see if they will go away of their own accord. I told him if he wanted to pursue the issue any further, it would take a lot of his time and effort, and he would have to be prepared for potential attacks. Troy said he felt the issue was so clear and important in his mind that he could not let it go.

I then asked Troy to define the issues as he saw them and to write a narrative of events that led to his being cut from the team. The two issues Troy felt very strongly about were that minority players were deliberately kept off the men's varsity basketball team and that his dismissal from the team had been a racially-motivated event. At my urging, he also collected five written statements from current and former men's basketball players that confirmed a racial factor was probably the reason for cutting Troy from the team. He put together what I considered to be an airtight case.

Troy took his appeal to the Interim President. Two mediation sessions, of which I was a part, were set up between Troy and the basketball coach. Both Troy and I felt, however, that the Interim President was unsympathetic to Troy's case. He didn't want to allow the written testimony of discrimination by the five other players because it was "hearsay." He wanted to reduce the issue to the coach and the player. He could then side, not unpredictably, with the coach. It was a blatant attempt to misuse power and to revictimize the one who had already suffered.

Troy had done his homework. He showed that when the coach came to the college in 1989, forty percent of the men's varsity basketball team was African-American. During the coach's term, the numbers had dwindled until Troy had been, for the last three years, the *only* African-American on the team. Then *he* was summarily cut. The coach claimed to have a different "recruiting strategy" from his predecessor. He preferred to recruit in the rural areas of the state, explaining that those were the kids who were "more likely to stay" than urban kids. The Interim President said he saw no significance to the figures showing a decline from forty percent minorities to zero percent in six years. He noted that lots of places have difficulties recruiting minorities.

The Interim President released his report on the situation eight weeks later, after promising to get it done in two. Not unexpectedly, he claimed to find "no evidence" of racial motive in the dismissal of Troy from the men's basketball team. Both Troy and I expected the verdict, but were disappointed nevertheless.

Rather than letting the matter drop, Troy next approached the local paper, which ran a front-page story on his situation. The response was instantaneous. As if on cue, many coaches and several players wrote rather vicious letters to the paper, claiming that since the coach was a Christian man, the charges of racism had to be groundless. People who had been Troy's friends for years began to ignore him. One college staff member who had said she was so proud of Troy now expressed enormous disappointment with him. Of course, no one addressed the mountain of evidence Troy had assembled. It was just too painful to believe that racism might have insinuated its ugly head into the safe confines of our little Christian college.

Seeing that Troy was getting unfairly berated in numerous letters to the editor, I carefully laid out the evidence in a lengthy editorial piece of my own. Several friends from a neighboring town, who had no connection to the college, considered it a "compelling" display of evidence. Yet my column sparked a depth of anger and vitriol that I did not think possible. I received obscene phone calls. A fellow professor, in violation of the faculty code, circulated a letter to every member of the community in which he tried to discredit me personally. In no instance did anyone refer to the evidence I had supplied.

During this time I decided I would have to leave the college. I received a three-year extension on my contract in March, but I couldn't sign it. I knew, instinctively, that by making an issue of this magnitude public, I had violated one of the most deeply cherished values: never, never, never let the world know this Christian college has anything wrong with it. I had broken a trust. I had enraged the students and faculty. There really was no choice but to leave.

Troy graduated in 1996, the same year I finished my teaching. Whether we accomplished anything in the long run remains to be seen, but someone in a high position (who was still talking to me) said later that major changes, were underway in the athletic department. I would like to believe that.

If I have learned anything through my reading of Martin Luther King, Jr., and my own foray into the area of racial justice, it is that there is a basic moral ambiguity to confrontative action. Confrontation may cause divisions that cannot be healed. The people accused will display an extreme form of moral indignation. There will always be people who think they know better than you what to do. Ambiguity arises from the fact that you don't *have* to confront. You can choose to ignore what you know, or to ask submissively and then let the matter rest if you don't receive a satisfactory answer.

Why endure the turmoil of confrontation? It is difficult to say. Sometimes there is the weight of the issue, sometimes lingering resentment over past hurts, sometimes the person doesn't even know why. But I believe King is correct when he says people in power don't willingly relinquish control. All the goodwill and reasoned argument in the world may fall on deaf ears. Then, and only then, does it become necessary to make the decision to confront.

In the end, there will always be those who second-guess the confronter. "It would have been more productive if you had waited, if you had gone through channels, if you had realized that I want changes as much as you, if you would trust God and the leaders God has given us, if you would learn the discipline of living with injustice, if you had worked a little harder to make the team." Many of these comments are good, cautionary pieces of advice for those who engage in confrontation. But most of them are offered by people who have never protested anything in their lives, and are spoken perhaps as much out of fear or ignorance as of genuine concern. In the end, those who practice social justice through the method of confrontation know they are accountable to their hearts alone.

Social Justice and the Ministry of Jesus

The biblical understanding of social justice is rooted in the Old Testament. Though the entire Old Testament bears witness to God's concern for the outcast and oppressed, the prophets were the leading spokespeople for social justice. Starting with Amos in the eighth century B.C. and continuing for several centuries, the Old Testament Prophets proclaimed the word of God to the people and the leaders of Judah and Israel. Unique among all their contemporaries in the ancient world, their authority was in their call from God, and their vocabulary included such words and concepts as "righteousness," "just dealing," "mercy," and "justice." They contrasted the call to justice with established religious practices of sacrifice and festival. The people of Israel may have been faithful to the latter, but they ignored the former. The prophets made it clear that unless the people repented and changed their behavior, the judgment of God would come down on them.

A few passages from the Prophets will demonstrate their intensity and emphases.

> I hate, I despise your festivals, and I take no delight in your solemn assemblies.
> Even though you offer me your burnt offerings and your grain offerings,
> I will not accept them;
> and the offerings of well-being of your fatted animals I will not look upon.
> Take away from me the noise of your songs; I will not listen to the melody of your harps.
> But let justice roll down like waters, and righteousness like an everflowing stream (Amos 5:21–24).

> "With what shall I come before the Lord, and bow myself before God on high?
> Shall I come before him with burnt offerings, with calves a year old? Will the Lord be pleased with thousands of rams, with ten thousands of river of oil?
> Shall I give my firstborn for my transgression, the fruit of my body for the sin of my soul?"
> He has told you, O mortal, what is good; and what does the Lord require of you but to do justice, and to love kindness, and to walk humbly with your God? (Micah 6:6–8).

> For I desire steadfast love and not sacrifice, the knowledge of God rather than burnt offerings (Hosea 6:6).
> Are you a king because you compete in cedar?
> Did not your father eat and drink and do justice and righteousness?
> Then it was well with him.
> He judged the cause of the poor and needy; then it was well.
> Is not this to know me? says the Lord (Jer. 22:15–16).

Is not this the fast that I choose: to loose the bonds of injustice,
to undo the thongs of the yoke, to let the oppressed go free,
and to break every yoke?
Is it not to share your bread with the hungry,
and bring the homeless poor into your house. . . ? (Isa. 58:6–7).

Jesus was certainly aware of the call to the prophets to proclaim social justice and to live in ways that exemplified it. He stood firmly in the prophetic tradition of Israel. Yet it is no simple matter to determine Jesus' "stand" or "position" on social justice.

The Ambiguity of Jesus on Social Issues

Jesus taught no clear-cut political or economic philosophy or theory of government and the state. Such a philosophy would include thoughts on the role of the state, the desirable forms of government, the rights and responsibilities of people, and the nature of government. An economic philosophy would include consideration of which system would best assure the production and distribution of goods, the stability of employment and the wealth of people.

Jesus has a way of confounding our categories. He fit into no convenient "pigeonhole" among the Jews of late antiquity, and even scholars today are hard-pressed to agree about the type of person he was. Early in his ministry, he developed a style that was quite different from John the Baptist and other religious teachers. So people began to raise questions about his actions. "Why do John's disciples and the disciples of the Pharisees fast, but your disciples do not fast?" (Mark 2:18). In other words, what is the purpose of having *disciples* if you have no *discipline*?

More frequent were questions about Jesus' associations. Why did he allow himself to be seen in the presence of tax collectors and sinners? On three occasions in the Gospel of Luke the religious leaders grumbled because "This fellow welcomes sinners and eats with them" (15:2; see also 5:30

and 19:7). Jewish religious teachers ought to have some respect for the Jewish purity codes. By associating with unclean or impure people, Jesus was causing discomfort for the religious leaders.

To make matters worse, when Jesus talked about certain subjects relating to social justice, some of his advice, if followed, might result more in *anarchy* than *order*. Consider his teachings on forgiveness and possessions.

> If anyone strikes you on the cheek, offer the other also; and from anyone who takes away your coat do not withhold even your shirt. Give to everyone who begs from you; and if anyone takes away your goods, do not ask for them again (Luke 6:29–30).

> Then Peter came and said to him, "Lord, if another member of the church sins against me, how often should I forgive? As many as seven times?" Jesus said to him, "Not seven times, but, I tell you, seventy-seven times" (Matt. 18:21–22).

Regardless of whether you agree it is possible to practice these things in your personal life, very few people would argue that these teachings ought to be social policy. No politician in America could espouse the first and hope to be reelected. Such a person would be labeled "soft on crime," and immediately his or her career would be over. Instead of three strikes and turning the other cheek three times, we have "three strikes and you're out" on felony crimes.

We are a society that increasingly wants to get people off welfare and other programs where the government supports able-bodied people. We have little compassion for beggars. Yet Jesus doesn't seem to endorse such policies. With respect to forgiveness, most of us excuse someone once or twice, but if the person hasn't gotten the message by then, our forgiveness stops. It is very difficult to translate Jesus' statements into a political or social philosophy.

One of Jesus' most arresting parables, the story of the laborers in the vineyard (Matt. 20:1–16), probes the issue of God's fairness and goodness. In this story a man hires laborers for the day to work in his field. He agrees to pay those hired early in the day the usual daily wage. The man hired additional workers at 9:00 A.M., noon, 3:00 P.M., and 5:00 P.M. to do the same kind of work as those first hired. At the end of the day (6:00 P.M.), he paid everyone. The ones who only worked an hour got a full day's wage—the same amount everyone else received. Those who had worked all day grumbled, "These last worked only one hour, and you have made them equal to us who have borne the burden of the day and the scorching heat" (verse 12). The employer responded, "Take what belongs to you and go: I choose to give to this last the same as I give to you" (verse 14). Though the parable is a beautiful story of the full grace of God given to those who "come to work" late for God, it does leave Jesus open to the question of whether there ought to be fairness in compensation among workers. It simply is an issue that Jesus did not comment upon.

Jesus was also a bit ambiguous in his teaching about wealth. On one hand Jesus seems quite adamant about the danger of riches. When the rich ruler wanted to follow him, Jesus said he must, "sell all that you own and distribute the money to the poor, and you will have treasure in heaven; then come, follow me" (Luke 18:22). When the ruler decided not to do this, Jesus exclaimed, "How hard it is for those who have wealth to enter the kingdom of God!" (verse 24)

Jesus also told about the rich man and Lazarus (Luke 16:19–31), where in the next life the rich man is plunged into torment while Lazarus feasts at Abraham's bosom. The story reveals a teaching we will return to below, that God will bring about a reversal of people's conditions in the future. In this instance, it appears that riches themselves are dangerous, a conclusion which seems to be supported by Jesus' teaching in the Sermon on the Plain: "Woe to you who are rich, for you have received your consolation" (Luke 6:24). Jesus' teaching is filled with warnings about the hazard of riches and the reversal of fortunes which the rich will face in the next life.

JESUS AND SOCIAL JUSTICE

But when one reads other sections of the Gospels, Jesus doesn't seem so concerned about the danger of wealth. The story of Zacchaeus (Luke 19:1–10) is a case in point. Zacchaeus was a wealthy, despised tax collector who wanted to see Jesus as he passed. Jesus saw him in the sycamore tree and invited himself to Zacchaeus' home. Zacchaeus spoke openly about his wealth and his desire to be a just tax collector. In response, Jesus declared that salvation had come to his house (verse 9). So here another standard is inserted. Wealth may not be entirely bad after all, even if it is acquired in a "shady" profession.

Finally, there is the confusing parable of the unrighteous manager in Luke 16 (verses 1–9). Fired because he squandered his employer's property, the manager shrewdly went to his employer's debtors and offered significant discounts on their invoices. By doing so, the manager got in the good graces of the debtors, which was good because he might have to "call in some favors" before long. The word got back to the employer who, instead of being enraged at the manager, praised him for acting shrewdly (Luke 16:8). The original word for *shrewdly* can also be translated "prudently" or "with foresight." Jesus commends the action of the manager by urging his disciples to "make friends for yourselves by means of dishonest wealth" (16:9).

Certainly Jesus' words are difficult and may never be satisfactorily explained, but they seem to suggest that the shrewd action of planning for his financial security after being fired was a worldly, but a praiseworthy thing for the manager to do. His point was that the children of the world outsmart the children of the light in this department. God's people should take a lesson from them and act shrewdly with respect to money also. So by comparing and contrasting all these teachings to Jesus, we have to conclude there was a certain ambiguity in regard to Jesus' teaching about wealth and its dangers.

Moving on to the topic of politics, let us briefly consider Jesus' attitude toward the Roman state, which was the occupying power in Judea and Galilee during his lifetime. What was his view of this occupation? Was it immoral? Justified? Irrelevant? Would he have supported the Zealots and Sicarii, fellow Jews who argued for a violent removal of the Romans? Would he have sided with the religious authorities who argued for collaboration with Rome? Would he have argued that it was irrelevant who ruled the land as long as the people could practice their religion? Each of these positions was well defended by Jews in the first century.

Jesus' first recorded words in the Gospel of Mark are laced with ambiguity, "The time is fulfilled, and the kingdom of God has come near; repent, and believe in the good news" (1:15). A politically inclined Jew could hear these words about the coming kingdom of God and conclude that Jesus was, in fact, inaugurating another Maccabean revolt. (The first one was launched by Judas Maccabeus in 167 B.C. and led to Jewish independence after 420 years of subjection to outside forces.) But those who were more spiritually minded could have interpreted Jesus' call in a personal or spiritual sense. They would assume Jesus meant for them to prepare their hearts for the coming of God. People hear the same words in dramatically different ways.

When Jesus was asked to clarify his position on Roman occupation, in the context of paying taxes to Caesar (Luke 20:20–26), Jesus nimbly handled the trick question. His opponents were trying to "trap" him into denying the authority of Rome. Nevertheless, when asked if it was lawful to pay taxes to the emperor or not, Jesus responded, "Give to the emperor the things that are the emperor's, and to God the things that are God's" (Luke 20:25). While I applaud Jesus' skill at avoiding such a "set-up" question, I am no closer to knowing his attitude toward the Roman occupation. Jesus appears to say that the Romans deserved *something* from the Jews, but what that something is remains ambiguous and elusive.

Clear Statements on Social Justice

I have already stated that the central value or message of Jesus was showing mercy and compassion. It is always the right time,

Sabbath or other day, to heal and help someone in need. In Jesus' famous parable about the last judgment, all the nations are gathered before God, and God separates the sheep from the goats. A major factor that determines the separation is how one has treated people.

> Come, you that are blessed by my Father, inherit the kingdom prepared for you from the foundation of the world; for I was hungry and you gave me food, I was thirsty and you gave me something to drink, I was a stranger and you welcomed me, I was naked and you gave me clothing, I was sick and you took care of me, I was in prison and you visited me. . . . Truly, I tell you, just as you did it to one of the least of these who are members of my family, you did it to me (Matt. 25:34–36, 40).

We have seen so many different phrases in the Gospels that indicate merciful action—being a neighbor, acting with compassion, showing mercy, doing good to the least of these, breaking down the barriers of race. These are a constellation of concepts, an explosion of suggestive phrases for the earnest disciples of Jesus. They provide us with clarity, variety, stories, and teachings, all leading to the same point—to love your neighbor as yourself. The key to Jesus' teaching on social justice, then, is to "be a neighbor," "be merciful," "love your neighbor as yourself."

One may be a neighbor and show compassion, but that is only a beginning. Also important to social justice are Jesus' teachings on *reversal* and his reaction to the Jewish leaders.

The theme of reversal of expectations runs throughout the Gospel of Luke, and appears as early as the song of Mary after her conversation with the angel Gabriel.

> His mercy is for those who fear him from generation to generation. He has shown strength with his arm; he has scattered the proud in the thoughts of their hearts. He has brought down the powerful from their thrones, and lifted up the lowly; he has filled the hungry with good things, and sent the rich away empty (Luke 1:50–53).

In Mary's sense of personal honor and exaltation at the news that she would bear Jesus, she realizes that God lifts up the lowly and humbles the mighty. That will be the promise of the Gospel.

Jesus affirms this in his Sermon on the Plain:

> Blessed are you who are poor, for yours is the kingdom of God.
> Blessed are you who are hungry now, for you will be filled.
> . . . But woe to you who are rich, for you have received your consolation.
> Woe to you who are full now, for you will be hungry (Luke 6:20–21, 24–25).

Reversal of position is a recurring theme in Jesus' early teaching.

This is also the point Jesus tried to get across to Simon the Pharisee (Luke 7:36–50). Simon had invited Jesus to dinner, probably hoping to impress, influence or find out more about Him. But an unexpected event interrupted their meal:

> A woman in the city, who was a sinner, having learned that [Jesus] was eating in the Pharisee's house, brought an alabaster jar of ointment. She stood behind him at his feet, weeping, and began to bathe his feet with her tears and to dry them with her hair (Luke 7:37–38).

The Pharisee, in this awkward moment, said to himself, "If this man were a prophet, he would have known who and what kind of woman this is who is touching him—that she is a sinner" (verse 39).

But Jesus responded to Simon's thoughts with a parable of two people who owed money to a creditor and who were both forgiven their debts. The point of the parable was to show that the person forgiven more loves more in return. In this case, the woman's awareness of her sinful condition was greater than Simon's. She showed more love for Jesus because she was forgiven more. She, the outsider, became a new insider. She would be included in Jesus' new community. Reversal would take place.

By telling this story, by healing outcasts, by putting people in their right minds, Jesus shifted the center of power in the world from those who *rule* to those who *know their need;* from those who are in powerful *institutional positions* to those who genuinely *seek forgiveness;* from those who *control* to those who *love.* He assembled his new community from those who were on the margins of life, because they were part of the great reversal which God was initiating.

This focus becomes even clearer in the stories about hospitality and feasts in Luke 14. Meals serve an important social function as well as a nutritional need. When we share food with one another, we also share our lives and a bit of our fractured and hopeful humanity. Meals have also been occasions to uphold or enhance social status. We might invite people to a meal because we "owe them one," we want to impress them or we hope to get to know them better. Seating at a meal, especially in political or diplomatic circles, is an art worthy of a Byzantine prince. So it is interesting that Jesus speaks about our "guest list" when we are preparing a meal.

Whom should we invite? Friends? Influential neighbors? Rich people? No. Jesus' instructions were to invite those who cannot return the invitation.

> But when you give a banquet, invite the poor, the crippled, the lame, and the blind. And you will be blessed, because they cannot repay you (Luke 14:13–14).

This is consistent with Jesus' earlier teaching about giving to those who have no possibility or means of repaying us (Luke 6:32–35).

Jesus went one step further in the Parable of the Great Dinner (Luke 14:15–24). A person planned a banquet and invited several friends, but soon the regrets came in. One had bought a new field; one had five new oxen; one had a new wife. They weren't willing to pull themselves away from their other commitments to attend this banquet. So the host ordered his servants to bring in the poor, crippled, blind and lame. As for those who were too busy to attend, he says, "I tell you, none of those who were invited will taste my dinner" (verse 24).

This parable symbolizes the banquet of the Kingdom of God. If people who have possessions, power, and distractions are simply too busy to respond to the call of God in their lives, they will be excluded from that banquet.

Jesus' teaching on reversal is really a critique of power and the ways it is expressed in society. Power has a pecking order, a finely calibrated system of measuring influence, a goal of getting to the top. Power is based on calculation and accumulation. Jesus knew that power frequently justifies ignoring the needs of people. He saw the cruelty of power exercised against "little" people. And his message was that such injustice would not always prevail. Someday, reversal would occur.

Jesus didn't provide a blueprint or a timetable of when the changes would take place. Yet by teaching about reversal, about bringing people from the edges of society to the center, Jesus fires the imagination and tests our hearts. When have we genuinely cared about bringing marginal people to the center? Have we ever used calculation as a means for assuring or promoting our advantage? When have we only given to someone on the condition of being repaid? Jesus' teaching on reversal is a judgment of our calculating ways, a critique of the values of civil society and an advance peek at the ordering of society in the kingdom of God.

These somewhat theoretical teachings on reversal are complemented by Jesus' harsh words against the Jewish religious establishment of his day. The most emphatic passages are Matthew 23 and Luke 11, but negative assessments of the scribes and Pharisees are sprinkled throughout the Gospels. Though a more detailed examination of Jesus' criticisms would be interesting, suffice it to say here that he indicted them for three major offenses: (1) they considered *profit* more important than *people;* (2) they held social *prominence* more significant than *people;* and (3) they focused on religious *particulars* to the exclusion of the needs of *people.* Here is but one example:

Woe to you, scribes and Pharisees, hypocrites! For you tithe mint, dill, and cummin, and have neglected the weightier matters of the law: justice and mercy and faith. It is these you ought to have practiced without neglecting the others (Matt. 23:23).

The focus on tithing insignificant items demonstrates their spiritual myopia. The Pharisees saw the trees but not the forest or, in the more arresting words of Jesus, "You strain out a gnat but swallow a camel!" (Matt. 23:24)

The more I reflect on Jesus' actions and teachings on social justice, the more clearly I see it is those who go along with the religious and political powers that be, those who affirm the status quo, who need to answer to Jesus. Why are we so reluctant to "make waves"? Why do we so easily go along with others when we don't agree with them? Is it because we, fundamentally, want to be liked? Are we concerned about our jobs, our safety, our comfort?

Perhaps we don't understand enough or think we know enough to raise questions. Perhaps we have so many other things clamoring for attention that we don't bother to consider things outside of our current reality. Whatever the case may be, the actions and teachings of Jesus on social justice make me vaguely uneasy with my life, causing me to wonder whether I have sacrificed my confession of Christ as Lord of my life to the expediencies and demands of today. Forgive me, Lord, when I do, and keep the picture of reversal ever before my mind.

Lord Jesus, there is pain in the world. There is suffering in the world. There are issues of racism in the world. This is an unjust world, Lord Jesus. People will die because of hunger. Children will die because of malnutrition. This is an unjust world. Jesus, stir within my heart a passion for justice. A passion to do what is right. A passion to follow and to do the truth of Jesus in a broken world. Stir within my heart Jesus, a desire, a commitment to stand up for those who are oppressed, to feed the hungry, and to love those who are broken hearted. Jesus, stir within my heart a commitment to pursue justice at any cost. Help me to understand it when I purchase gas. Help me to understand it when I walk into the market and buy food. Help me to respond to it when I desire to buy clothes which are cheap because of the exploitation of children who are underpaid and overworked in a system which only recognizes material gains. Help me to see it and understand it when I watch CNN and see the pain of those who are dying because of unjust laws. Let me pray and pursue the acts of justice, both within and without my own community, in the name of Jesus. Amen.

8

JESUS AND THE FORMATION
OF THE NEW COMMUNITY

> When the Stranger says: "What is the meaning of this city?
> Do you huddle close together because you love each other?"
> What will you answer? "We all dwell together To make money
> from each other"? or "This is a community"? O my soul, be
> prepared for the coming of the Stranger, Be prepared for him
> who knows how to ask questions.
>
> —T. S. Eliot, *Choruses from "The Rock"*

When Phil Jackson became head coach of the Chicago Bulls in 1989, he inherited a team with Michael Jordan, perhaps the greatest player in the history of professional basketball. Yet it was a team that had never even come close to winning an NBA title. If Chicago were to win a championship, Jackson saw he would have to mold the players into a team rather than a motley collection of individuals who stood around admiring the fantastic moves of Michael Jordan. Jackson would have to change the philosophy of the team and emphasize that each player had an essential contribution to make to the success of the team. He laid out this approach in his autobiography, *Sacred Hoops: Spiritual Lessons of a Hardwood Warrior.*

One of his first tasks was to speak with Michael Jordan, who had just finished one of the most amazing seasons of individual accomplishment since Wilt Chamberlain in the

1961–62 season. Jackson told Jordan that if the Bulls were to win a championship, Jordan might have to sacrifice five points per game from his scoring average in order to involve the rest of the team. Jordan may even risk losing the NBA scoring title if the Bulls were to win the NBA crown. Jordan, being the class athlete that he is, decided to give Jackson's philosophy a try. Central to Phil Jackson's plan was the creation of an environment that would make each player see how his success was integrally related to his ability to help his teammates succeed. The results of this approach have been stunning: three consecutive NBA titles in 1991–1993, fourth and fifth titles in 1996–1997 and the best regular-season record in NBA history during the 1995–96 season. Along the way the Bulls have discovered rare gifts in players thought to be irredeemable, such as Dennis Rodman, and have built a world following for the game of professional basketball.

A different type of team building is described by Kathleen Norris in her book, *The Cloister Walk*. Norris is a writer who left the New York literary "hothouse" in the early 1970s to return to the homestead of her maternal grandmother in Lemmon, South Dakota. For more than twenty years she has been chronicling her life and the lifestyle of small communities in the high plains. As her spiritual yearnings intensified, she found herself (a Protestant) being drawn to the Benedictine community of monks and nuns at St. John's University in Collegeville, Minnesota. She became an "oblate" of the monastery, which means that she took as many vows of monastic discipline as she could, being a married woman living apart from the community. Twice she lived at the monastery for nine months, seeing faith and community from a new angle. Her insights about life in a monastery are eye-opening, but most revealing for my purpose here are her comments on what holds a monastic community together.

Monks, she tells us, are like everyone else. They feel anger and lust, pride and envy. They battle sloth, greed and gluttony as they try to live faithfully. Often in a monastic community, some of the most trivial things become the source of grudges between people. As one monk said, "Our biggest problem is that each man here had a mother who fried potatoes in a different way" (p. 21). Great tensions exist between structure and freedom, diversity and unity, openness to the world and retreat from it. Yet beyond all the tensions are some bedrock commitments of the monastery, some non-negotiables which define the very essence of the members. These may be defined as the centrality of worship, humility, solitude and community. If these priorities are preserved and nurtured, the community will live and flourish, despite the eccentric and sometimes bothersome ways of its members.

In both of these settings, a successful professional sports franchise and a Benedictine monastery, the value of the community or team is the bedrock of the enterprise. The emphasis on community acts as a healthy check on the rampant individualism that has seeped into every pore of American life. From youth we are taught the importance of our *own* achievements, our *own* accomplishments, our *own* uniqueness. In our electronic age each worker becomes autonomous, able to take his own files, desk, money and duties wherever he goes, and do his work wherever he happens to be. We equate freedom with autonomy in our culture, freedom from having to put up with other people, freedom to drive our own car down whatever road we choose into the sunset.

Not so with Jesus. Though he called and healed individuals, he called them into a community of faith. He poured his life into a select group of disciples so they would continue his vision after he was no longer with them. He created a community, called the body of Christ, which has hands and feet, legs and fingers, toes and arms. If one member rejoices, all rejoice together. If one member weeps, all are sad. Jesus found his life fulfilled in a community and bids us to do the same. The goal of this chapter is to understand the nature of this new community which Jesus created. We will examine the bedrock principle of the new community and living life in the new community.

Forgiveness: The Bedrock Principle
of the New Community

The fundamental principle of the new community Jesus called into being is forgiveness. Without forgiveness there is no community. Like Jesus' disciples then, we today need forgiveness because of the burden, the baggage, or the guilt which we carry. I was powerfully reminded of such a burden during a conversation on a recent flight I took across the country. I sat next to a distinguished-looking retired gentleman who greeted me warmly. As we soared above the clouds, I learned a little of his story.

He was seventy-five years old and was a lawyer who had spent several years as Chairman of the Board of an East Coast bank. He talked about his family and life, his vineyards in California and his activities during his retirement. As we continued to talk, however, I detected a deep sadness in his voice. I inquired about it and discovered he was still carrying a lot of pain from his pre-retirement years. He mentioned that even though others considered him to be a successful man, he knew, in the core of his being, that he wasn't. He said, "When I attained a high position at the bank, I had an image of myself as a good and fair man, accessible and just in my dealings with all people. But in my position I began to make decisions that hurt people, families and even communities. I had to make the decisions; it was as if I were being carried along by a wave over which I had no control. I saw myself becoming a cold and unfeeling person, even as I was leading the bank in profitable directions. As a result, I neglected my inner life, the voice of conscience that told me to return to my earlier values. But I simply could not do so.

"I came to see that my perception of myself as a good man was disappearing. I carry a lot of emotional scars because of the people I hurt. I neglected myself and hurt others. As a matter of fact, I feel rather dead inside." And then, looking wistfully out the window as we approached our California landing, he confessed, "I cannot even enjoy the taste of the grapes and wine from my own vineyard."

I saw next to me a man of immense spiritual yearning who bore a load of guilt, a burden that seemed to crush him and take away his enjoyment of life. Even though he radiated health and confidence, he had become dead inside. He needed a deep cleansing and sense of acceptance, an assurance that he could be released from the burden which weighed down his soul. In a word, he needed forgiveness.

The need to be forgiven and freed from a load of guilt can occur at any age. A middle-aged doctor and his wife came to speak with me one evening. He was successful in his field and, from all external measures, in most other things in life. The couple had four attractive and healthy children, all of whom were beginning to make their way in the world. Only recently had the doctor discovered some of the cost of his success. His older son, twenty-one years old, had been attending college for three years with no particular direction or career interest in mind. The son had recently developed a drinking problem, and had even been picked up for driving under the influence of intoxicants. His parents had done everything from gently encouraging him to seek counseling to threatening to with-hold all support from him in order to coax him back to a more healthy course of life.

But during these times, the son would lay a "guilt trip" on the parents that went something like this: "Dad, you have always been there with money, but not with yourself. You were so concerned with building your career when I was little that you never came to my games. You never were there for me. You never gave me the direction and encouragement I needed. And now that I need your help, you are threatening to cut me off."

Even though the parents were smart enough to know that their son was blaming them in order to get them to "lighten up," the father was still numb. He said, "I understand what my son is doing to me, but I have to confess, I feel my inadequacy. The truth is, I *wasn't* there for him; I *was* building my career. I often spent sixteen to eighteen hours a day for weeks on end trying to establish a practice. I *know* I neglected my son and I felt guilty about it, but fifteen years ago I figured I had no other choice. Now it has come home to roost, and my worst nightmare has come true."

Many people have similar stories. Behind nearly every iron fence and shaded driveway is a story of life desperately lived, of guilt that grips and will not let go, of the need for forgiveness from terrible burdens that sap the energy from otherwise healthy people. We might live in an age of psychoanalysis where guilt is seen as an unhealthy remnant of a repressed age, an unsightly boil that needs lancing by the sophisticated language of science. But the solution is not that simple. We also live in an age which has created its own pleasures of the body and mind which seemed so exhilarating and harmless at the time but which, in fact, are crippling our bodies and minds today. This generation bears a different kind of scars than its ancestors. Our ancestors, working in the dangerous mines, the dreadful mills or the unforgiving soil, bore physical scars. We, in our high-tech world, with lithe bodies and intact limbs, bear the invisible scars of incredible *internal* pain. We are as vacant internally as the huge abandoned shells of old industrial buildings which occupy the urban wastelands of every city in this country. We need someone to ease our pain, to tell us not to fear, to touch us in a way that will relieve the pain and lighten the burden of guilt. We need forgiveness today.

When we turn to the Gospels and look at how Jesus defines the new community, we see how central the principle of forgiveness is. Let us examine three biblical stories which show the importance of forgiveness in the ministry of Jesus and for the formation of the new community.

The Call of Peter (Luke 5:1–11)

Jesus was standing by the sea teaching. The crowd, having witnessed his remarkable acts of healing, pressed in on him.

So he got into a boat, skippered by Simon, and asked him to push off from shore where he could have a convenient and safe place to teach the crowds.

When Jesus stopped speaking to the people, he told Simon to cast his net into the sea. Simon protested at first, but then complied:

> Master, we have worked all night long but have caught nothing. Yet if you say so, I will let down the nets (Luke 5:5).

Simon expected to bring up an empty net, but it was so full that it almost broke with the weight of fish. Another boat pulled alongside to help, and even then the two boats began to sink. As his boat was sinking, Simon sank to his knees and spoke:

> When Simon Peter saw it, he fell down at Jesus' knees, saying, "Go away from me, Lord, for I am a sinful man!" (Luke 5:8)

This story reveals a number of important insights. First, this is the only occasion in the Gospel of Luke where Simon's whole name (Simon Peter) is used. It is a hint to the alert reader that something about the *whole person* is going to be revealed in the conversation with Jesus. The name reveals the character; something of Simon Peter's character will come out soon.

Also important is the strong reaction Simon Peter has to Jesus. Rather than saying, "Thanks, Jesus," or "I love you, man!" or some expression of gratitude for this unexpected economic boon, Peter said, "Go away." Actually, the Greek word is much stronger. It is the same word used throughout the Gospels by Jesus when he is casting out demons from an afflicted person. So, really, the meaning is closer to "Begone!" "Leave me alone!" "Get lost!" Peter's words had a tone of urgency, of desperation. He was immediately aware that the great catch of fish reflected a *spiritual* force which had been released, so he responded with *spiritual* language: "Go away!"

Why would Peter have reacted so strongly, so insistently, so discourteously? Why was he so overwhelmed by Jesus' act? He must have realized that if Jesus had so much knowledge, so much inner perception about Peter's own specific area of expertise, then how much more must he know about the things of the spirit! Jesus awed Peter with his immediate and deep knowledge of the things most important to Peter. How much more, then, did Jesus know of Peter. How much more, then, must he know of who *I* am?

David wrote Psalm 139 from a perspective of faith and gratitude, but Peter might have recited it from the perspective of sadness and desperation. This is how Peter felt!

> O Lord, you have searched me and known me.
> You know when I sit down and when I rise up;
> you discern my thoughts from far away.
> You search out my path and my lying down,
> and are acquainted with all my ways (vverse 1–3).

While the psalmist says, "Such knowledge is too wonderful for me" (verse 6), Peter would say "Such knowledge is unbearable for me!" Some of the following thoughts may have flashed like lightning through Peter's mind: *I know I am a sinner. I am not worthy of you. I know that no good dwells in me. So do you, Jesus. I am just a simple fisherman. Leave me alone. Let me live my life as an obscure man. Go and choose your disciples from those much more talented, more educated. I just do not have the personality to be one of your followers. I am not your man! Get lost!!*

These thoughts are summarized with the simple phrase, "Go away from me, Lord, for I am a sinful man!" Jesus, undeterred, responded, "Do not be afraid; from now on you will be catching people" (Luke 5:10). "Do not be afraid" means the same thing as, "Your sins are forgiven." It was Jesus' way of saying, "Simon Peter, I can handle whatever you bring to me. If you realize that I know you thoroughly, then you must also realize that I know you better than you know yourself. I can see in you the seed of fidelity and strength, of steadiness and determination. I can use a man with those qualities."

When Jesus says, "From now on you will be catching people," he is really saying that he will transform Peter's abilities. It is a remarkable claim. Jesus is saying that it is "from now on" that matters. Peter's past, which made him shrink in fear at the Lord's feet and beg for him to leave, need not hound him anymore. I believe that little information is provided about the disciples' "pre-discipleship" days because ultimately, in Jesus' eyes this is unimportant. The important thing is what comes "from now on."

Simon Peter needed to hear that, and so do we. We live in an age where psychology is the dominant profession that deals with one's interior life. Psychology has given us untold riches and insights in this century, and many insights come from the realization that your past shapes your present. Until you learn to "deal" with the depths of your past, you are not free to live today and tomorrow. While not wanting to discount that advice, which has helped so many people, I believe we are in a time of change in our culture. Now that we know we are shaped by our *past,* what we really need are resources for the *future.* We need a Savior who can examine our lives and help us live "from now on." Only then can we get beyond our abusive past, our dysfunctional families, our addictions and griefs. The Apostle Paul stresses the same point when he says, "So if anyone is in Christ, there is a new creation: everything old has passed away; see, everything has become new!" (2 Cor. 5:17)

Jesus pointed Simon Peter to the future. "From now on you will be catching people." Jesus transformed Simon Peter's fishing ability into a new realm. Catching people. How catchy. And why not? With the old inadequacies forgiven, the uncertainties removed, the guilt wiped away, why not look to the future with expectation and hope? Forgiveness would be the foundation of Simon Peter's life; it would enable him to live "from now on," to "catch people," to live for Jesus. Later, in Simon Peter's darkest days when he betrayed his Lord and wept bitterly over his failure, it was the power of forgiveness that restored him to the community. Forgiveness possesses a strength, a suppleness, a potency that does not simply bring people into the Lord's community, but keeps them there, strong and deeply rooted, able to withstand the fiercest storms of life.

The Healing of a Paralytic (Luke 5:17–26)

Forgiveness and new life were not limited to the twelve disciples; they were gifts that Jesus offered to all wherever he went. A story from the early days of Jesus' ministry brings this out clearly. The man's condition and the situation of his friends is described in Luke 5:18–19:

> Just then some men came, carrying a paralyzed man on a bed. They were trying to bring him in and lay him before Jesus; but finding no way to bring him in because of the crowd, they went up on the roof and let him down with his bed through the tiles into the middle of the crowd in front of Jesus.

People in need were thrusting themselves on Jesus from all angles. The friends of the lame man showed their resourcefulness by removing a roof and lowering their friend right into Jesus' presence. Peter may have thought Jesus was "in his face" but we now see an example of how people were, literally, "in Jesus' face." It is interesting that the lame man seems to be a non-entity in this story. He is carried, he says not a word, he gives no indication of support or opposition to this scheme of his friends. He lies there on the mat—passive, motionless, inert.

Jesus perceived this. He saw the persistence and ingenuity of the friends and then spoke to the man. The text says, "When he saw their faith, he said, 'Friend, your sins are forgiven you'" (Luke 5:20).

Note the language. When Jesus saw *their* faith, the faith of the friends, he then spoke to the man. Faith is an integral part in healing, but in this case it was the faith of others which Jesus recognized. But why were Jesus' first words to the man, "Your sins are forgiven you"?

Jesus saw that in spite of the man's physical disability, his *spiritual* condition was a deeper problem. Physical lameness was a sign, in this case, of spiritual weakness. The fact that he had to be carried by his friends was an indication that he felt like a burden to them. What is it like to feel that you are a burden to other people or to yourself? You can't take care of yourself, you can't live independently, and at any moment of the day you might require the presence and assistance of another person. By being a burden to others, you prevent them from living their lives fully.

Helplessness frequently lead to feelings of guilt. You wish you didn't have to be a burden, but you have no choice. You feel guilty because you cannot forgive yourself for making others' lives miserable. This kind of guilt can lead to passivity, to grim resignation, to embarrassment whenever you face your friends or family. The paralyzed man was carrying a larger burden within his soul than his friends were carrying by taking him to Jesus.

That is why Jesus addressed him with the words, "Your sins are forgiven you." Jesus knew the man needed to be released from his spiritual burden. If that could be accomplished, certainly his physical condition could be remedied as well! How surprised and gratified the man must have been to hear himself addressed as a spiritual being! He knew, deep in his soul, that his tangled limbs were an indication of the tangled depths of his heart. Finally, here was a man who understood him, who knew that his spirit could still be vital. Here was a person who could heal his spirit, straighten out all the tangled realities within, restore his wounded soul, wash, cleanse, purify, and satisfy the deepest longings of his heart. Here was a man who would forgive, pardon, let him start anew.

If I am pardoned, he must have thought, *I no longer have to condemn myself. I no longer have to be my own judge, jury and prison warden, locking myself deeper and deeper away from human connections. I can stop punishing myself for being a burden to others. Maybe, just maybe, I can feel free again. It is almost too much to hope for.*

But Jesus then said, "I say to you, stand up and take your bed and go to your home" (Luke 5:24). Oh, what words! Immediately strength coursed through the man's dead limbs, and a charge like an electrical current was activated, enabling the man to leap up and praise God.

Forgiveness is real. Outer strength mirrors the newfound strength of the soul. The forgiven person is joyful, energetic and expressive. Thanks be to God!

Forgiveness in the Community (Matt. 18:15–35)

One of Jesus' most important rules for community life had to do with discipline and forgiveness. The practice of forgiveness is placed in the context of church order. Whenever it comes to disciplining wayward members, people want to know what the ultimate sanction is. Human nature just wants to know what will happen in a "worst-case" scenario. So Jesus gave rules about what to do if members simply refuse to abide by the decisions of the church (Matt. 18:15–18). But then he shifted the emphasis from those who offend to those who are sinned against. The focus changed from *them* to *us*. Jesus centered his teaching on forgiveness *not* on how one deals with the sinner or offender, but how we act and live after being offended. His point is that being sinned against is a great opportunity *not* to straighten out someone else's life, but to practice the noblest of Christian virtues, forgiveness.

Jesus' unusual perspective raised a question in Peter's mind:

> "Lord, if another member of the church sins against me, how often should I forgive? As many as seven times?" Jesus said to him, "Not seven times, but, I tell you, seventy-seven times" (Matt. 18:21–22).

Peter thought he was being gracious. Forgive a person seven times? That sounded like a pretty heroic action, an example of gracious living. But Jesus' response, regardless of whether your Scripture translation reads "seventy-seven" or "seventy times seven," was really a way of telling Peter that he had asked the wrong question. By putting the words "how often" and "forgive" in the same sentence, Peter showed he still didn't understand the heart of the Gospel. It is like asking a doctor, "How many breaths should I take each day?" It is a question that is wide of the mark, because forgiveness needs to be as natural and common to the church as breathing is to a person.

Jesus continued by telling the Parable of the Unforgiving Servant (18:23–35). A king decided to punish a servant for the incalculable debt he had run up. But when the servant threw himself on the mercy of the king, his debt was canceled. Yet that servant then turned around and demanded that a fellow servant pay off a small debt. When the fellow servant could not pay, the first servant had him thrown in prison. The king heard about the unjust treatment shown by the one he has forgiven, and quickly imprisoned the offending servant "until he would pay his entire debt" (verse 34). The parable echoes the words of Jesus just after the Lord's Prayer: "For if you forgive others their trespasses, your heavenly Father will also forgive you; but if you do not forgive others, neither will your Father forgive your trespasses" (Matt. 6:14–15).

Three brief points that come out of this parable: (1) the absolute necessity of forgiveness; (2) the short duration of forgiveness; and (3) the penalty for failing to forgive. Forgiveness is necessary because we have been forgiven so much. Those who are forgiven little, love little. Those who recognize the depth of God's forgiving work in their lives, love much. (See also Luke 7:36–50.) Forgiveness allows us to start life anew, fresh, today. The past is no longer held against us and need not control us. Forgiveness cleans the slate that has become dirty and soiled over the years. Forgiveness lets us breathe again with joy.

Since God gives us the chance to start again, we must extend that same opportunity to each other. Remember that the emphasis is on those who have been offended. Give another chance to those who offend you, since God forgives you time after time.

Second, the effect of forgiveness, from the human perspective, is fairly short-lived. This is a painful but true point. The servant who was forgiven much quickly turned on the one who owed him very little. The forgiveness that meant so much to him a moment before wasn't passed along. Practicing forgiveness is like trying to keep a house clean in the Midwestern dust bowl. You can mop and dust, but the cleanliness doesn't last. You'll have to do it again the next day. Practicing forgiveness is like riding the ferris wheel at the state fair. While you are soaring high above everything else, you have an exhilarating feeling of freedom and limitless potential, but when the ride is over, so is the feeling. Practicing forgiveness is like making resolutions. They may last a day, week or month, but rarely longer. Genuine forgiveness requires hard work. We need to understand that in our human weakness, we need to extend forgiveness to people every day. Our own shortcomings should remind us to forgive others.

Finally, failure to forgive leads to dire consequences. In the parable, the servant was thrown into jail and would not be released until he had paid everything. The person who does not forgive is like someone in prison. He or she is in a cage, captured and tormented by all kinds of evils. Such a person nurtures grudges, ponders how to get vengeance, and becomes preoccupied by the other person. Conversely, the person who knows how to forgive is truly free. The real test of church discipline, then, is the ability to forgive someone—not just once, but as often as needed. That is the strength of the Christian community and the foundation of the new community which Jesus created.

Life in the New Community

Jesus called his disciples "to be with him, and to be sent out to proclaim the message, and to have authority to cast out demons" (Mark 3:14–15). The first requirement is often overlooked, but is the most essential: to be with Jesus. The key to the life of discipleship is to share a common life and support each other in moments of strength and weakness, hope and sadness, anger and delight. Discipleship is something that is *caught* more than *taught,* so it was essential for Jesus' disciples to "be with him."

Jesus assembled a unique and diverse group. Though we don't know much about the lives of the disciples, we can infer from the New Testament that they had widely different personality traits and political affiliations. Matthew was a tax collector, an occupation despised by many Jews because it supported the Roman overlords. Simon was referred to as a Zealot, which was the political party dedicated to removing the Romans by any means necessary. Peter was impetuous, hot-tempered, quick to jump to conclusions. John was the beloved disciple, reflective, calm, even mystical. Jesus didn't seem to be aware of the modern principle of church growth, articulated in the 1970s and 1980s, that homogeneity is the basis for growing churches. He seemed to cultivate diversity, even potential conflict, in his movement.

As we see the disciples interact with Jesus, two contrary but true realities develop. The first is the *ignorance and infidelity* of the disciples, and the second is Jesus' growing *desire for intimacy* with them. These two realities are in tension throughout the Gospels. In order for the movement to succeed, to outlast its founder, the disciples have to learn the essentials, so Jesus pours himself into them. But the more he teaches them, the more confused, unfaithful and undiscerning they seem to become. Yet the more unfaithful they become, the harder he tries to connect deeply with them. At times Jesus' frustration is evident—"You faithless generation, how much longer must I be among you?" (Mark 9:19) In the end, he does the only thing he can, which is to trust his disciples and to commend his spirit into the hands of a gracious God.

Ignorance and Infidelity

A lot of ignorance can be excused. The disciples were called to follow someone who would redeem Israel, whom they believed was the Messiah, yet there were contrary and incomplete expectations of who the Messiah would be and what he would do. They needed to be educated, and Jesus was willing to do so. But at times the disciples seemed impervious to instruction, unable to learn the simplest lessons of faith.

After a day of healing, casting out demons and teaching, Jesus sailed with his disciples toward the other side of the lake. He was so tired that he soon fell asleep in the boat. When a storm began to rage, the panicky disciples woke him with the words, "Teacher, do you not care that we are perishing?" (Mark 4:38) Do you not *care*? Jesus had spent many days showing his compassion for all kinds of people. How could the disciples suggest that Jesus didn't care? After rebuking the sea, Jesus turned and rebuked his disciples, "Why are you afraid? Have you still no faith?" (Mark 4:40) Faith seemed to leave them as quickly as the effects of breakfast. Their faith seemed fragile, uncomprehending, weak.

A short while later, after Jesus had multiplied bread and fish to feed the 5,000, he retreated to pray. The disciples rowed across the sea, encountering much difficulty because the wind was against them. Jesus caught up with them, walking on the sea. They saw him, but were terrified. Jesus got in the boat and stilled the wind. The text says:

> They were utterly astounded, for they did not understand about the loaves, but their hearts were hardened (Mark 6:51–52).

It wasn't long before the disciples' lack of understanding was again the focus of a talk with Jesus. Twice Jesus had multiplied bread to meet the needs of thousands of people. But when Jesus tried to warn his disciples of the "yeast" (teaching) of the Pharisees, they speculated, "It is because we have no bread" (Mark 8:16). They missed the point completely! Jesus was not talking about the quality of the loaves produced by the Pharisees' bakery, but rather the insidious nature of their teaching. Yet the disciples remained uncomprehending. They were tied to material reality, to their immediate physical needs. They couldn't read the signs of the times or even the nuances of Jesus' words. Finally, in frustration, Jesus asked, "Do you still not perceive or understand?" (verse 17) In other words, "Don't you see that I am the bread of life, the true nourishment of your lives?" But there was no response, not even a glint of recognition of what he was talking about.

Just before Jesus made his final journey to Jerusalem, he asked his disciples who they thought he was (Matt. 16:13–20). Immediately Peter replied, "the Messiah." Encouraged by this flash of insight, Jesus talked about his upcoming suffering. Peter, impulsive as ever, began to rebuke Jesus, as if Jesus didn't understand his own destiny. Jesus, in some of the strongest language that ever passed his lips, said:

> Get behind me, Satan! You are a stumbling block to me; for you are setting your mind not on divine things but on human things (Matt. 16:23).

During the last few days of Jesus' life, the disciples added infidelity to their ongoing ignorance. Jesus was in the Garden of Gethsemane asking God if the cup of suffering might pass from him, sweating as if it were great drops of blood, and needing all the support that friends can provide. Where was the inner core of his disciples? They had fallen asleep waiting for him. When Jesus was on trial in the high priest's palace, Peter emphatically denied he knew him. When Jesus was on the cross, in his most vulnerable and painful moment, his disciples had already fled. Mark writes of "women looking on from a distance" (15:40). But few of the brave, defiant, strong men were to be found. Ignorance, infidelity, insubordination, incompetence, indolence, incapacity, ineptness, incredible dullness. *That* was the track record of the first disciples.

Intimacy with the Disciples

The fact that Jesus kept trusting and training his disciples is one of the truly amazing examples of his love. Early in his ministry, Jesus was more reluctant to entrust himself to his followers (John 2:24), but as the end drew near, he drew his disciples ever closer into his confidence. John 13–17 describes a scene of growing intensity and true intimacy between Jesus

175

and the disciples. During this time he empowered the disciples for service when he would no longer be with them.

As the time neared for Jesus to return to God, he gave the disciples an *example* and a *commandment*. The example was the washing of the disciples' feet as Jesus demonstrated true servanthood. The command was for the disciples to love one another: "By this everyone will know that you are my disciples, if you have love for one another" (John 13:35).

Then Jesus moved from the realm of example and commandment to focus on *knowledge*. The disciples needed to know a few things before he left them. The first thing the disciples needed to know was the unity of Jesus with God the Father.

> Believe me that I am in the Father and the Father is in me; but if you do not, then believe me because of the works themselves (John 14:11).

Jesus had made the same statement to the crowds earlier (10:38), but they tried to arrest him for saying it. Now, in the intimate confines of the upper room, he again emphasized this truth to his disciples.

A second thing his disciples needed to know was that Jesus would soon send the Spirit, who would lead them into all truth. One of the truths the Spirit would affirm was Jesus' unity with the Father.

> On that day you will know that I am in my Father, and you in me, and I in you (John 14:20).

Notice the new element added here. Not only is Jesus in the Father, but we (his disciples) are in him. As if to stress that point, he goes on to say:

> Those who love me will keep my word, and my Father will love them, and we will come to them and make our home with them (John 14:23).

176

These words form the basis for the most intimate and powerful image of the vine and the branches in John 15, where Jesus gives one of his famous "I am" statements:

I am the true vine, and my Father is the vinegrower. He removes every branch in me that bears no fruit. Every branch that bears fruit he prunes to make it bear more fruit (John 15:1–2).

Then, in the space of seven verses (15:4–10), he uses the word "remain" or "abide" eleven times to stress the intimate connection we as disciples have with him. The key to life is "abiding" in Jesus. Other translations of that word are "remaining," "dwelling," or "staying." One verse that captures the heart of Jesus' words is John 15:5:

I am the vine, you are the branches. Those who abide in me and I in them bear much fruit, because apart from me you can do nothing.

Though John never defines the word "abide" in this passage, at least three things are implied. First, to abide means that *we draw our life from Jesus.* If forgiveness is to be a daily activity, as important to us as breathing, we must learn to abide in Jesus. We who abide realize that Jesus is absolutely essential to our lives. We cannot exist without him. Peter realized this early in Jesus' ministry after Jesus had frightened off many people with some harsh-sounding words. Jesus asked the Twelve, "Do you also wish to go away?" Simon Peter responded, "Lord, to whom can we go? You have the words of eternal life" (John 6:68). When we can affirm with Peter that Jesus' words lead to eternal life, then we have learned the secret of abiding in him.

Second, to abide in Christ means that *we bear fruit for him.* The branch draws its life from the vine and yields fruit to the world as a result. The fruit we should bear is described nicely by the Apostle Paul:

The fruit of the Spirit is love, joy, peace, patience, kindness, generosity, faithfulness, gentleness, and self-control (Gal. 5:22–23).

The indwelling Christ shapes the lives of disciples, working intimately in the intricate depths of our hearts, to make us more Christ-like, more able to instinctively reflect the character of Jesus.

The product of our fruit-bearing is the discovery of new abilities.

Very truly, I tell you, the one who believes in me will also do the works that I do and, in fact, will do greater works than these, because I am going to the Father" (John 14:12).

Finally, the result of our abiding is that we have a restored *prayer life*. Jesus promised:

If you abide in me, and my words abide in you, ask for whatever you wish, and it will be done for you" (John 15:7).

Consistency in prayer is the sign of one who abides in Jesus. Recall that we defined prayer in chapter 4 not so much as a continuing activity of asking, but of listening and enjoying the presence of God. By abiding in Christ, we luxuriate in the strength and nourishment he pours into our lives. We drink deeply of his life-giving waters. We meditate on the truths of his Word. We live with hope, joy and love in the world. We confidently know that our destiny is to be with him.

When our prayers and requests are attuned to the Spirit of Christ which dwells within, the requests are granted. The previous verse is not a blanket statement to "ask for anything" as if God is some kind of Santa Claus who will give whatever we request. It is, rather, an encouragement to draw deep nourishment from the vine so that Christ's life becomes our life. Consequently, Christ's desires become our desires. This kind of intimacy assured the disciples of long ago. We today can also face the future unafraid. As Jesus said:

I have said this to you, so that in me you may have peace. In the world you face persecution. But take courage; I have conquered the world!" (John 16:33)

With this kind of Lord on our side, what fear should we have? Any incompetence or infidelity is washed away by the intimate longings for Christ within us. Thanks be to God!

⌁

Thank you lord Jesus that I am a part of a community. A community of people called up by faith, a community of people who have been forgiven. People who understand their need for you and are intricately connected to your love. Jesus, this community that I am a part of is multicultural, multiethnic, and is made up of people of different skin tones, different languages, and different backgrounds. We all have something in common: OUR NEED FOR YOU. Thank you that I am a part of a new community. May I live out the values of that community in my every day life. May I be free from any racism or sexism or any other spirit of prejudice that would hinder the growth and development of a new community. May I be free from any slander that would affect my commitment to a new community. Thank you Lord Jesus that I am part of this new community. Amen.

9

JESUS AND SUFFERING

I said to my soul, be still, and let the dark come upon you Which
shall be the darkness of God. . . . So the darkness shall be the
light, and the stillness the dancing.

—T. S. Eliot, *Four Quartets*

I am writing this chapter just a week after the tragic mid-air
explosion of TWA Flight 800 and the death of 230 passengers
and crew off the coast of Long Island, New York. The grim search
continues as the most advanced technology is used to comb the
ocean floor for clues to the explosion. Tearful relatives and friends
are at a loss to explain the tragedy. Their tears are mingled with
accusations; their vulnerability is evident to every witness of their
private holocaust. In Montoursville, Pennsylvania, where sixteen
members of the French club and their five advisors perished in
the crash, life will never return to normal. In a moment, in a
twinkling of an eye, thousands of people immediately became
grief-stricken. Disaster has left its merciless signature on the sur-
vivors and has blown apart their lives with the same lack of compassion the original blast showed to the passengers and crew.
Tragedy has etched itself on their souls as distinctly as their fingerprints are imprinted on their hands.

Our advanced technology and instantaneous communication
capabilities seem to provide a hospitable environment for disasters to occur. They appear quickly on our television screens and
disappear almost as quickly as they are replaced by other events.

Of course there are the natural disasters, which have existed since time immemorial, such as floods, earthquakes, fire, and great storms. But there are also human-induced disasters and suffering, ranging from the meltdown of a poorly constructed and monitored nuclear reactor in Chernobyl, to the bombing of the Murrah Federal Building in Oklahoma City. In addition, there are war disasters of small or epic proportion which often don't sink deeply into our consciousness because we have no bard, no modern Homer, to sing us the pain of these wars. We have seen the greatest humanitarian tragedy in a generation, beginning in 1994 in Rwanda, rekindling long-standing hatred between Hutu and Tutsi. Genocide and massive acts of human cruelty are only gradually coming to light in the aftermath of the Yugoslavian Civil War of the early 1990s. Throughout the world immense suffering is taking place because long-standing hatreds are being unleashed. History might be a resource from which to extract principles of peace between people, but it can also become the mine from which ancient hatreds are drawn out and reignited in our world.

And only the worst suffering makes the headlines. We hear little about the quiet deaths in intensive care units, the silent desperation of AIDS sufferers, the estrangement and sadness that stalk so many lives, the utter hopelessness and brokenness of uncounted millions. These tragedies also quietly contribute to the world's unmeasurable "suffering index." We have devised all sorts of methods to measure human employment, success, financial health, and hopes for the future, but no survey can accurately measure the intensity, depth and persistence of human suffering and pain.

Life is such a mixed plaid, such a painful gift. If we extend ourselves widely to form broad networks of friendships, our joy is apt to be fuller, but so will be our suffering. If we decide, on the contrary, to limit our connections to others, attempting to create a buffer between us and the suffering of others, it doesn't work. We are made for relationships that can provide depths of passion and love, yet they can also suck every ounce of vital energy from us.

Jesus was no stranger to suffering. He was a "man of sorrows and acquainted with grief." The sorrows he faced were not simply due to his empathetic capacity; that is, they did not occur simply because he identified with the pain of others. He had his own share of losses and disappointments, his own confusion and sense of abandonment by God, his own seeming inability to make his life "work" in the way that others could understand and support. In this chapter I will examine the nature of Jesus' suffering and death, and try to explain how his suffering can be redemptive and instructive for us today.

But I need to make three points about suffering before looking at the life of Jesus. These points emerge from my reading and reflecting on suffering and the human condition, and should shed light on the discussion of Jesus and his suffering.

The first comes from the Reynolds Price book, *A Whole New Life,* which describes his life-changing struggle with a devastating tumor on his spinal column. He writes, "You're in your present calamity alone, far as this life goes." He does *not* mean there is no comfort in suffering, no presence of God, no help from friends. My point is that when the lights are off, when the greetings and good-byes have ended, and perhaps even in the midst of the pleasant company of helpful people, you are alone. There is no one, earthly or heavenly, who will pull you out of your illness. The sensation is something like being alone on a long stretch of western highway where there is just you and the silent and majestic world of nature. In suffering *you* are the one who must develop a strategy to deal with the pain, with the doctors and nurses, with your family and friends, with God. Once the tidal wave of suffering hits, you are the only one who can put together the resources to understand and resist it. During such times of great aloneness there will also be times of great grace and unexpected joy, but you must learn to interpret them and put them in context.

Second, suffering frequently has no discernible purpose or meaning. People try to "soften the blow" of suffering by providing explanations during and after the event. You've heard such attempts: "Things could have been worse." "Suffering builds a deeper life." "Suffering is an essential element for spiritual growth." "Suffering often brings out the best in people."

But when all is said and done, suffering usually has no reason. It is absurd. The root meaning of *absurd* is "deaf." Something absurd has no explanation that any person can hear. Suffering works against every human inclination to protect, nurture and live fully.

Third, suffering can at times be the instrument of great grace. If one emerges on the far side of suffering and survives the crises of body and spirit, suffering actually can result in new levels of hope and joy. As the Apostle Paul says,

> We also boast in our sufferings, knowing that suffering produces endurance, and endurance produces character, and character produces hope, and hope does not disappoint us, because God's love has been poured into our hearts through the Holy Spirit that has been given to us (Rom. 5:3–5).

Suffering can provide an uncanny sense of what is true. It creates a rawness of experience by which to test other experiences and a capacity to cut through life's fluff and red tape to get to the nub of the issue. Suffering may enlarge one's capacity to listen and learn, to identify lessons and teachers, to form intimate partnerships with new people. Suffering may be the doorway to a rich, satisfying, deep life which has its own unique rhythms, contours and joys. The community of those who suffer may appear to be twisted, tangled, and gnarled, watered by the wellsprings of a million tears. Yet it is a blessedly twisted community, discovering triumph amid tears, toughness amid the tangle, and grace among the gnarled and helpless limbs.

Suffering and the Life of Jesus

As we examine suffering in the life of Jesus, we will not confine ourselves to the last week of Jesus' life or to the physical and mental agony of the cross. We will see a more richly textured narrative of Jesus' suffering that includes his physical and mental life, and which involves much more of his life story. Just as the diseases that afflict us are often slow-growing and only come to our attention after many years, so Jesus' suffering was deeply entwined with his life. We will look at the following aspects of suffering and the life of Jesus: (1) Jesus' Growing Consciousness of His Aloneness; (2) A Hopeful Vision; (3) Facing Betrayal and Crucifixion; and (4) Triumph through Suffering.

Jesus' Growing Consciousness of His Aloneness

Jesus knew his call from God was to heal and to teach, to proclaim the year of the Lord's favor (Luke 4:18–19). He knew he would call a group of disciples to be with him whom he could teach and equip to carry on his great renewal movement. Jesus' life, from the time of his baptism, was lived among numerous people. Often he was so hard-pressed that he needed to withdraw and rejuvenate himself, but his withdrawal was always for the sake of returning to the ministry. He wasn't interested in being a hermit, a desert monk fighting the devil and praying for the salvation of the world. Indeed, he fought the devil and prayed for the world, but he also involved himself in the world, teaching, healing, and showing compassion to people. Yet as he spent time with people and poured himself into his disciples, he realized the depth of his aloneness.

He was alone and solitary for three reasons: he had alienated the people in power, he was misunderstood by even his closest companions, and he realized, in a powerful way that he only partially communicated, the compelling strength of the biblical role he was to fulfill with his life.

I have already addressed the alienation of the religious leaders and the misunderstanding of his disciples. But before mentioning the third point, I need to add here that I am troubled by the notion of Jesus being misunderstood by almost everyone during his ministry. As a teacher for more than twenty years, I know that misunderstanding is frequently a two-way street. If I am univer-

185

sally misunderstood when I try to make a point, I can assume that *I* am partially to blame for the confusion. Either I have not been clear, I have not prepared the students for the point I am making, or I am not exactly sure what I am trying to say. But perhaps we can explain the gap between Jesus' words and people's lack of understanding with the following story.

One of the most influential philosophers of education in the twentieth century was John Dewey (1859–1952). Dewey is without peer in his concern for child-centered education, experiential learning and democratic values in all levels of education. Early in his teaching career at Columbia University, he was a powerful lecturer, animated and articulate, earnest and energetic. It was almost as if he were possessed by an outside force as he talked about education. But according to one of his colleagues, the only problem was that no one seemed to understand a word he said! The young Dewey was compelling, but incomprehensible. I believe the problem was the combination of *too much* knowledge and *too much* desire, all needing to be expressed *right now*. Dewey was too far ahead of his peers.

So it's no wonder that Jesus was misunderstood. He had *so much* to say and such a deep heart. The simple people who witnessed his healing and heard his teaching needed years to absorb and understand his message. But Jesus didn't have that much time. He had time to accomplish the work he had come to do, but not to explain all the hows and whys to the people who were with him. Jesus overloaded time with the weight of his words. Consequently, they faced frequent confusion and misunderstanding.

We return to the third point above, the compelling strength of a new biblical picture. Beginning with the days surrounding his baptism, he carried around two images of his work: king and servant. You should recall that in his initial sermon at his home synagogue, he referred to these images in the light of Isaiah 61:1–2, as he declared that his work was to set captives free and proclaim the year of the Lord's favor. With this mission in mind, he set about healing and teaching, casting out demons and preaching. The new and powerful biblical picture of the prophet who heals and proclaims, like Elijah or Elisha, seemed to shape his self-understanding.

But as opposition developed, Jesus realized that the prophetic vocation throughout Israel's history was one that led to rejection and death. He seems to have combined his emphasis on prophet with the picture of servant of God. He will be a prophetic servant or a serving prophet. The deepening antagonism with religious leaders provided the occasion for Jesus to deepen his understanding of himself as the unique servant of God. The concept of the servant of God is a tremendously rich one in the Book of Isaiah, described in four passages. Space does not permit a complete examination of these passages, but here is a brief summary:

- the servant proclaims justice (42:1–4)
- the servant becomes a light to the nations (49:1–7)
- the servant's humiliation at the hands of his enemies (50:4–9)
- the servant's brutal punishment, death, and vindication (52:13–53:12)

Jesus drew his self-understanding at this point of his ministry primarily from the last of these passages.

What I am claiming is that as the opposition to Jesus increased, he remembered God's words at his baptism, and began to see his life increasingly in terms of the servant of God described in Isaiah. This servant had a prophetic message to proclaim, to be sure, but Isaiah made it clear that the servant would give his life to set others free.

If one studies the language of Isaiah 52:13–53:12 closely, one is struck by how difficult many of the phrases are to translate. It is almost as if the author was so overcome by the treatment of the servant that he could barely hold his pen straight to write. As Jesus increasingly saw his life in terms of the servant of God in these passages of Isaiah, we can understand how he might struggle to comprehend how the words of the prophet would intersect and apply to his life. We can also understand why the disciples and others couldn't understand Jesus, even when he spoke clearly about his upcoming suffering. The passage and image on which he was drawing was among the most difficult in the Old Testament. He had not previously used the "suffering servant" image in his teaching and healing. And Jesus was far ahead of the disciples in wrestling with the certainty that his life would be sacrificed for the redemption of many.

As Jesus' understanding of his role as the servant of God grew, the disciples' understanding waned. They could understand healing; they could even grasp some of his teaching. But, when their master began to refer to an obscure passage about suffering, dying and rising again, it was just too difficult to grasp. As they sank deeper into incomprehension, Jesus became more alone. But now it was an aloneness nurtured by the deep nuances of the Word of God, a spring of life-giving water which would slake his thirst from Galilee all the way to the Garden of Gethsemane.

So Jesus increasingly understood himself in terms of the servant who would be exalted but marred beyond human semblance (Isa. 52:13–14), who would be despised and rejected by people (53:3), who would bear the infirmities and carry the diseases of all (53:4), who would bear the punishment that others deserved (53:6), who would be oppressed and afflicted but silent (53:7), who would be taken away by a perversion of justice (53:8), yet, in the end, who would be vindicated and satisfied (53:11–12). The servant of God has to go all the way with God. He could not stop with simply proclaiming justice, going to the nations with his message, or even giving his back to his smiters. He had to go the distance, finish the race, bear the cross and then wear the crown. This thought was, for the disciples, strange, novel, unprecedented, unexpected. When Jesus told them that he had to suffer, it is no wonder that Simon Peter impetuously responded, "God forbid it, Lord! This must never happen to you" (Matt. 16:22). It was the sober truth, but few people, including the disciples, could grasp it.

A Hopeful Vision

Suffering can seem like descending into a huge, dank, unlit cave. The walls are close, we can't see what's ahead, we have little comfort, and we cannot determine a way out of our dilemma. Suffering limits and blurs our range of vision. We become absorbed by it, consumed by it, even intoxicated by it. We are especially vulnerable just after learning of a serious physical problem. We think the worst even as we hope for the best. During such times all of our senses are open to receive insight, and all of our inner receptors are straining for messages, for meaning, for knowledge into our condition. At this time in Jesus' life, I believe he received a message of confirmation and strength. I will discuss Jesus' suffering after putting it in the context of a more current story.

Earlier in this chapter I referred to author Reynolds Price. For more than thirty years he has written novels and plays, many of which have won national awards. He has also been a part-time professor of writing at Duke University in North Carolina. In 1984, at age 51, he learned that he had cancer. Doctors found a ten-inch-long tumor twisting around his spinal cord. Apparently the tumor had been there for years. The first symptoms Price experienced were his uncertain steps and the loss of feeling in his legs. When his doctor discovered the tumor, he grimly announced that it was the largest such tumor in the history of Duke Hospital (Price wondered, at first, whether he deserved some kind of award). He needed immediate radiation treatment at the maximum dosage. The attempt to kill the tumor would unfortunately kill the surrounding healthy cells as well. His prospects for recovery—and even survival—looked grim indeed.

Just before the radiation treatment started, while Price was at home in bed, he had a curious experience. At a point between sleep and consciousness, he had a vivid vision or dream of Jesus and healing. He had never considered himself a religious man, even though he believed that God created him and guided his life. Because of the power of his account, I reproduce his exact words here:

> I was suddenly not propped in my brass bed or even contained in my familiar house. By the dim new, thoroughly credible light that rose around me, it was barely dawn; and I was lying fully dressed in modern street clothes on a slope by a lake I knew at

once. It was the big lake of Kinnereth, the Sea of Galilee, in the north of Israel—green Galilee, the scene of Jesus' first teaching and healing. I'd paid the lake a second visit the previous October, a twelve-mile-long body of fish-stocked water in beautiful hills of grass, trees and small family farms.

Still sleeping around me on the misty ground were a number of men in the tunics and cloaks of first-century Palestine. I soon understood with no sense of surprise that the men were Jesus' twelve disciples and that he was nearby asleep among them. So I lay on a while in the early chill, looking west across the lake to Tiberias, a small low town, and north to the fishing villages of Capernaum and Bethsaida. I saw them as they were in the first century—stone huts with thatch-and-mud roofs, occasional low towers, the rising smoke of breakfast fires. The early light was a fine mix of tan and rose. It would be a fair day.

Then one of the sleeping men woke and stood. I saw it was Jesus, bound toward me. He looked much like the lean Jesus of Flemish paintings—tall with dark hair, unblemished skin and a self-possession both natural and imposing. Again I felt no shock or fear. All this was normal human event; it was utterly clear to my normal eyes and was happening as surely as any event of my previous life. I lay and watched him walk on nearer. Jesus bent and silently beckoned me to follow. I knew to shuck off my trousers and jacket, then my shirt and shorts. Bare, I followed him.

He was wearing a twisted white cloth round his loins; otherwise he was bare and the color of ivory. We waded out into cool lake water twenty feet from shore till we stood waist-deep. I was in my body but was also watching my body from slightly upward and behind. I could see the purple dye on my back, the long rectangle that boxed my thriving tumor.

Jesus silently took up handfuls of water and poured them over my head and back till water ran down my puckered scar. Then he spoke once—"Your sins are forgiven"—and turned to shore again, done with me.

I came on behind him, thinking in standard greedy fashion, "*It's not my sins I'm worried about.*" So to Jesus' receding back, I had the gall to say, "Am I also cured?"

He turned to face me, no sign of a smile, and finally said two words—"That too." Then he climbed from the water, not looking around, really done with me.

I followed him out and then, with no palpable seam in the texture of time or place, I was home again in my wide bed (*A Whole New Life*, 42–43).

This event, this vision, took place at the beginning of a most harrowing time of Price's radiation therapy, recovery, numerous relapses, loss of use of his legs, near-death experiences, and finally, gradual stabilization as a paraplegic. Price considers the vision a gift from God to stabilize and strengthen him through the long, dark tunnel of his upcoming suffering. He wrote, "I've believed that the event was an external gift, however brief, of an alternate time and space in which to live through a crucial act" (p. 44).

I believe a similar event in Jesus' life was his transfiguration (Luke 9:28–36). The story is placed, significantly, directly after Jesus first announces that he must die:

> He sternly ordered and commanded them not to tell anyone, saying, "The Son of man must undergo great suffering, and be rejected by the elders, chief priests, and scribes, and be killed, and on the third day be raised" (Luke 9:21–22).

Jesus was aware that as the servant of God, he *must* suffer. He was beginning the long journey through the uncertain tunnel of anguish and pain. Shortly after the announcement of his impending death, he ascended the mountain with three disciples to pray. While there, his appearance changed and his clothes became dazzling white.

> Suddenly they saw two men, Moses and Elijah, talking to him. They appeared in glory and were speaking of his departure, which he was about to accomplish at Jerusalem (Luke 9:30–31).

Jesus saw two notable figures from the past, Moses and Elijah, who spoke with him about his upcoming departure at Jerusalem. The Greek word translated "departure" is, literally rendered, "exodus." This is its only appearance in the New Testament, and it is a word rich with biblical associations. The exodus of the people of Israel from Egypt was an event of departure, to be sure, but it also marked the birth of the nation. Without the exodus, there would have been no giving of the law, no promised land, no kingship and prophecy, no messiah. Exodus meant liberation and freedom; it meant the end of the hard road of brick-making and subservience to a cruel and uncertain master. The Exodus was the beginning of life for Israel.

Therefore, when Moses, the leader of the Exodus, and Elijah spoke to Jesus about his upcoming "exodus" at Jerusalem, their conversation would carry the overtones of the *beginning* of life and not the end, the *birth* of a people and not the death of the leader. Certainly Jesus, the servant of God, would face punishment and death, but he could justify the meaning of that event in his own mind as a time of liberation and freedom for the people of God. Perhaps Moses helped explain to Jesus that his upcoming death was not the end, but really the start of God's new relationship with his people. Moses could speak from experience.

And what about Elijah? Almost all scholars interpret Elijah's presence as a sign that the end of time is imminent. Elijah's presence was predicted "before the great and terrible day of the Lord comes" (Mal. 4:5). Therefore, according to this interpretation, Elijah's presence is an announcement that the end is near. While there may be some truth in that interpretation, I see Elijah's presence significant in a different way. Elijah was one of the few people in the Old Testament who never died. He was taken into heaven in a fiery chariot (2 Kings 2:11). Elijah could talk with authority about the great transition between life and death and what it means to be caught up into the presence of God.

The purpose, then, of Moses and Elijah, was to provide a sense of deeper knowledge and comfort to Jesus in his time of need. As we will see in the next section, Jesus needed all the strength that such a vision would provide. With the reality of this vision in his mind, he could "set his face" to go to Jerusalem (Luke 9:51). Nothing would deter or deflect him from his path. He moved toward Jerusalem as the servant of God who would suffer, but with the confidence that his suffering would really be an "exodus," the beginning of life for many.

Facing Betrayal and Crucifixion

The suffering of Jesus intensified during the last few days of his life. Many of the events are described in Mark 14–15. It is not only a narrative of betrayal, trial and crucifixion, but also a chronicle of deep internal suffering, increased abandonment and near-monumental despair. Any hope accumulated during the previous conversation with Moses and Elijah would certainly be stretched thin.

Jesus' suffering was, without doubt, physical. Many scholars have described the cruel ravages of crucifixion, the nails ripping at flesh, the lungs bursting, the death by strangulation as one becomes unable to draw another breath. Yet, as the story unfolds, we discover the depth of Jesus' mental and spiritual torment was perhaps deeper than the physical suffering. Jesus' frequent references to the psalms of distress in this passage suggest that only those most desperate, wrenching writings could possibly provide a context for his suffering.

But we must raise a more precise question about Jesus' spiritual or mental torment: what exactly caused it? It was not simply due to betrayal, abandonment, the futility of defending himself against trumped-up charges, or kangaroo-court-style justice. I think at the heart of Jesus' suffering was the *gradual stripping away of Jesus' dignity, the steady erosion of any sense that his life had any worth at all.* One may be able to endure physical pain, but the mental anguish of humiliation combined with the spiritual torment of having every shred of dignity unceremoniously torn away becomes too much to bear. It leads to abject hopelessness.

A story from my trip to Saudi Arabia in 1993 might help to make the point clearer. That Middle Eastern culture is no doubt closer to Jesus' culture than is life in modern America. What I learned on my trip was the centrality of honor as a cultural value for Middle Eastern societies. I saw it in the greetings the Saudis gave to one another. As our guide would lead us, a delegation of thirteen American professors, around the cities of Jeddah or Riyadh, he would often encounter people he knew. For several minutes he and his acquaintance would greet one another with hugs, kisses, and phrase piled upon phrase. Later I asked my guide what they said to each other. He told me they were literally searching their minds for every phrase they knew that would honor the other person: "Greetings to the jewel of Jeddah, the crown of the region, the man whose family brings honor to the entire kingdom." Honor and the recognition of honor are the *real* oil that lubricates Middle Eastern societies.

I saw also the "shadow side" of honor when two women from our group were able to interview some Saudi women who had taken the unprecedented step of driving a car in Saudi Arabia during the Gulf War. The women wanted to highlight the plight of all Saudi women and sought this visible symbol as a way to evoke international support for their quest for additional rights. Now, two years later, these women were asked, "What was the reaction to your act?" The Saudi women tearfully recounted how the incident had been perceived within the Saudi framework of honor and dishonor. They had dishonored their families in just about the most serious manner possible. They had embarrassed their country and had put themselves ahead of the interests of their families and clans. As a result, they were denounced by name in public religious ceremonies. Their husbands, fathers and brothers were shunned by the community. It would take years before the breach of honor, caused by this incident, could be repaired.

I think stories like these help put Jesus' experience during the last days of his life into a better context. His humiliation resulted from the theft of his dignity by all kinds of people. I will highlight several incidents from Mark 14–15 to show the gradual stripping of dignity which Jesus faced prior to the complete humiliation of the cross. The growing crescendo of Mark 14 leads to the triple fortissimo of the crucifixion in Mark 15. If we sense the rhythms of the narrative, we can better understand Jesus' growing desperation.

As Jesus shared the Last Supper with his disciples (Mark 14:12–31), he broke the festive mood of the occasion with a somber statement:

Truly I tell you, one of you will betray me, one who is eating with me (verse 18).

His statement evoked sorrow and consternation from the disciples and inserted a tone of sadness to the gathering. After the meal, they went to the Mount of Olives, high above the old city of Jerusalem to the east. Then Jesus dropped a second bombshell:

You will all become deserters; for it is written, "I will strike the shepherd, and the sheep will be scattered" (verse 27).

What Jesus predicted here was desertion, not betrayal. It is the difference between intentionally pushing a person off a cliff and not trying to rescue someone who is about to fall. In this case Jesus said they all would abandon him. Just think of it—at a crucial time, all would fail the test. If that isn't a reason for self-doubt in a teacher, nothing would be.

To make matters even worse, all denied Jesus' assertion, with Peter being the most vocal. He said:

Even though all become deserters, I will not (verse 29).

"*I* will stand firm. *I* will be faithful. *I* am not like these other disciples who will abandon you at the crucial moment and leave you in the lurch. *I* will accompany you to the end." That is the sentiment of Peter, a feeling that is curiously like the statement of the proud Pharisee when he said, in contrast to the tax collector:

God, I thank you that I am not like other people: thieves, rogues, adulterers, or even like this tax collector (Luke 18:11).

In this case, it was the tax collector rather than the Pharisee who went home justified.

Peter's protestation of fidelity must have intensified Jesus' sense of aloneness and eroded his dignity even further. Peter misjudged himself badly. The vehemence of his denial added to the sadness of Jesus. Imagine what Jesus must have thought: *You just don't get it, do you? You can't read the events that are unfolding right before your eyes. And when all of you say you will be faithful, it is nearly overwhelming. Where have I gone wrong? Why can't any of you see?*

Jesus' agony increased when he went to pray in the Garden of Gethsemane with Peter, James and John. He wanted to reconcile himself to his own death in the midst of clear signals that the disciples, his closest associates, perceived nothing of the reality that was upon them. The words from Mark's Gospel are very powerful:

He took with him Peter and James and John, and began to be distressed and agitated. And he said to them, "I am deeply grieved, even to death; remain here, and keep awake" (14:33–34).

Commentator William Lane says about this passage:

The urgency of Jesus' instruction was underscored by his experience of shuddering horror. The suffering which overwhelmed him is forcefully stated: he was "appalled and profoundly troubled," and spoke of a depth of sorrow which threatened life itself. The unusually strong language indicates that Mark understood Gethsemane to be the critical moment in Jesus' life when the full meaning of his submission to the Father confronted him with its immediacy (Lane, William L., *Commentary on the Gospel of Mark*, 516).

Jesus had to submit with dignity after all his dignity had been eroded. He could just as easily have said, "Who cares anymore? It is worth absolutely nothing! I am the doormat of all. You too, God, might as well demand that I am your doormat too! It would be consistent with the treatment that I have received so far!" Yet with great dignity and a strong sense of self, Jesus expressed his desire to avoid this ordeal, but also reinforced his willingness to follow God's will. His flesh and his heart may fail, but God was still the stronghold of his life.

In this powerfully moving scene, Jesus reached for words that would express his sorrow, and he chose a psalm of distress. He said, "I am deeply grieved." Another translation is, "My soul is cast down," which is a direct reference to Psalms 42 (verses 5, 11) and 43 (verse 5). Three times in the two psalms the psalmist searches to discover, "Why are you cast down, O my soul, and why are you disquieted within me?" He wanted to offer praise, but he could not. His present reality was expressed in Psalm 42:7: "All your waves and your billows have gone over me."

The same reality of being submerged, cast down, and grief-stricken, was true of Jesus in Gethsemane as he prayed while his disciples slept.

Then came the act of betrayal (Mark 14:43–50). Jesus had predicted it, had seen it unfold, and at this point it reached its horrible conclusion. He was betrayed with a kiss.

Let him kiss me with the kisses of his mouth!
For your love is better than wine (Song of Solomon 1:2).

Solomon's song speaks of the kisses of love, but Judas' kiss was another kind of greeting. It was a despicable imitation of an act of true intimacy, a perversion of the meaning of the act itself. Pathos piled upon pathos as Jesus' dignity was stripped away further. Jesus quoted no Scripture, but he could easily have referred to Psalm 55, a psalm of betrayal, in this context:

It is not enemies who taunt me—I could bear that;
it is not adversaries who deal insolently with me—I could hide
    from them.
But it is you, my equal, my companion, my familiar friend,
with whom I kept pleasant company; we walked in the house
    of God with the throng.
Let death come upon them; let them go down alive to Sheol
    (verses 12–15).

Once again, the Psalms capture the depths of despair and internal anguish that the betrayed person must have felt.

When a person suffers distress and seeks the face of God for relief, sometimes he or she discovers that more grief is on its way. Suffering has an awesome capacity to devour us, even when we think we are completely consumed. When we have reached the bottom of the Pacific Ocean, and think we can go no deeper, we discover the Marianas Trench, a narrow slit on the floor of the ocean that plunges several thousand feet deeper into the core of the earth. We reach what we think is the bottom, yet are sucked even deeper.

Similarly, Jesus' distress continued to deepen. He faced trumped-up charges and humiliation at the hands of the high priest's henchmen (Mark 14:53–65). False witnesses arose and tried to play on the prejudices of the crowd: "We heard him say, 'I will destroy this temple that is made with hands, and in three days I will build another, not made with hands'" (Mark 14:58).

The witnesses didn't agree, but that didn't matter. The point was to humiliate Jesus. Eventually they "discovered" that Jesus had blasphemed God, so they unleashed their hatred by striking, taunting, and spitting on him.

Did anyone come to the rescue? Of course not. Peter had an opportunity (Mark 14:66–72), but as Jesus predicted, Peter denied three times that he knew Jesus. Rather than standing with Jesus, his friends and followers folded like cardboard. The final words of Mark 14 stress that the unreliability of Jesus' accusers had become credible because the only credible witnesses had been discredited by malice and cowardice. The world had been turned upside down.

Finally there was the crucifixion and death of Jesus (Mark 15:21–39). It was preceded by the mocking of the soldiers and the taunts of the crowd. When Jesus was hanged on the cross (the tree) he became accursed. The Law of Moses explains:

> When someone is convicted of a crime punishable by death and is executed, and you hang him on a tree, his corpse must not remain all night upon the tree; you shall bury him that same day, for anyone hung on a tree is under God's curse (Deut. 21:22–23).

So Jesus waited to die—nailed to a cross, abused by the people, cursed by God and abandoned by his disciples. The whole world, as it were, seemed to shout "No!" at him. The words of Lamentations must have been on his heart:

Is it nothing to you, all you who pass by? Look and see if there is any sorrow like my sorrow, which was brought upon me, which the Lord inflicted on the day of his fierce anger (Lam. 1:12).

We do know that in this time of deepest alienation, Jesus again recalled the psalms. This time he chose a psalm of complete desolation which precisely matched the forsakenness of his soul. It was Psalm 22, and note the bleakness of the opening lines:

My God, my God, why have you forsaken me?
Why are you so far from helping me, from the words of my
groaning?
O my God, I cry by day, but you do not answer;
and by night, but find no rest (Ps. 22:1–2).

Some scholars, seeking to preserve the dignity of Jesus and cushion the blow of his anguish, assume that he began to recite the whole psalm, which ends with words of praise and hope. But I think by this point, Jesus was so weak and his mind so clouded that only the first few verses, if that, came to mind. He was dying abandoned, alone, reviled. The nails ripping at his flesh were symbolic of the sword that pierced his inmost soul. The horrible truth is that he died in despair.

Triumph through Suffering

Even if crucifixion had been the last word, people still might have been able to start a religion with Jesus as its central figure. It could have been a movement of martyrs, who would throw themselves before the juggernaut of the Roman Empire or any oppressor as a witness against cruelty in all its forms. But such a movement, in addition to being extremely small, could do nothing to affirm life or demonstrate that life, rather than despair, will have the last word. The unexpected, glorious and riveting truth of the Gospel is that crucifixion, death, suffering and despair are *not* the last words. In the words of a hymn set to the music of J. S. Bach, "The victory belonged to life."

One of my favorite Scripture verses on this theme is Isaiah 53:11 in the Revised Standard Version translation. I am sure I will take this verse in my heart to my grave. Its precise words are:

He shall see the fruit of the travail of his soul and be satisfied.

The servant of God is promised vindication. Satisfaction, rather than despair, will be the fruit of travail. Delight, liberation of others and salvation will be the last words of life.

I won't elaborate here, but there are three ways in which this satisfaction emerges at the end of the Gospel story. First, Jesus' divinity was recognized by a Roman soldier present beneath the cross. When the centurion saw that Jesus had died, he said, "Truly this man was God's Son!" (Mark 15:39) This is not to be interpreted as a confession of faith in Jesus as the Messiah but rather an instinctive realization of the Roman soldier that the person before him was divine. The first person who truly recognized the divinity of Jesus was one who was sworn to uphold the Roman system. More Romans would soon make the same confession.

Second, the cowardly disciples and the women who watched from a distance gradually returned to assess the damage and affirm their shaky faith. Like families returning to a burnt-out house or a neighborhood devastated by earthquake or fire, they came gingerly, quietly, tearfully, confused, fearful, and bewildered. They joined each other in a silent vigil, waiting for something that may never come, that they may never recognize. They were together, however, and they shared their sadness and maybe even their hope.

Finally, and most importantly, there was the resurrection of Jesus on Easter morning. Death could not hold him. And though the first appearances of Jesus were met with more confusion and fear, Jesus had time to calmly explain to his disciples about himself, to remove their misconceptions, to promise the gift of the Spirit, and to empower them for the ministry which lay before them. Jesus' immense suffering resulted in immense satisfaction—unexpected, riveting, life-changing. Go, tell it on the mountain!

Death is destroyed, is swallowed up by life! Death will no longer have the last word. Pain is transformed into hope; suffering is transmuted into joy.

✦

Lord Jesus, why do I run from suffering? Is it something within my own culture and my own upbringing that hides from any form of suffering? And yet you say unless I take up my cross and follow you daily I do not really have life. I run from the cross and there are times when I feel ashamed of it, because to suffer means that I would identify with those who are less fortunate than myself, and those who are less powerful than myself. And yet, Lord Jesus, if I do not identify with those, then I have no part of you. So Jesus, let me receive you, let me receive the cross, let me receive the truth of the cross. Help me to care and be committed and reach beyond myself and to identify with those who are less fortunate, who are in pain, and who struggle. I take on the cross Lord Jesus. Teach me its implications. Teach me its values that I might live a life of truth. Amen.

CONCLUSION

PART FOUR

THE LIVING JESUS SPEAKS

10

A Lifetime Burning
in Every Moment

Time past and time future What might have been and what
has been Point to one end, which is always present. . . . a lifetime burning in every moment . . .

—T. S. Eliot, *Four Quartets*

U ntil now we have been concerned with the "inner" and
"outer" life of Jesus. We have examined the sources of his
inner strength and the pattern of his life in the world. We have
rediscovered Jesus and have seen him as a human, compassionate, intuitive, independent, thoughtful and focused person. We have tried to better understand his teaching, stories,
healings, and feelings of abandonment.

In the final chapter we will raise a question that we have not
yet posed, but which is crucial to understanding and following Jesus today. It is a question that will require some imagination and speculation to answer, but it is asked by every pastor and serious student of Jesus' life today. What would Jesus
say to us today at the end of the twentieth century? If Jesus
were alive, in the flesh, what might he tell us?

In trying to answer this question, I want to deal with four
points: (1) The Inherent Dignity of All People; (2) The Challenge of Race; (3) The Snare of Greed; and (4) Living from
the Heart.

The Inherent Dignity of All People

On occasion I share my Christian faith with some of the broken and less fortunate people in my community. Every city has more than enough people who fit this description. At present, I am the pastor of a new church development for the Christian Reformed Church, Centrepointe, in suburban Grand Rapids, Michigan, but I also find myself drawn to the inner city, the place of my own roots. Recently, before a trip into the city, I prayed, "Lord give me the eyes of Jesus to see and respond to the needs of your people. Let me see as you see."

I drove to one of the poorer sections of town, ironically called Wealthy Street, and began to talk to the people. One conversation with a middle-aged woman is memorable to me. I asked her what she felt was her greatest need. I was surprised when she began to weep. She said she had just returned from the bridge, where she had been contemplating suicide. She was particularly oppressed now because her fourteen-year-old daughter had been caught selling drugs. The court appearances were coming up. The mother had debated long and hard whether she should end it all, but had decided not to because of a promise she had made to her grandmother.

Then, in labored but clear words she said, "I need someone to tell me that I am worth something. I need someone to look me in the eye and say that I am a person of dignity, that I have worth, that I have value in this world." I was cut to the heart and I vowed silently that I would let her cry echo as widely as possible. It was the cry of a burdened heart, pushed almost to the breaking point. She could have said, with author Zora Neale Hurston, "I have lived in sorrow's kitchen and licked out all the pots."

I think the first thing Jesus would say to us today is that all people have an inherent dignity that needs to be recognized and embraced. I can hear Jesus saying, "You may talk about the inherent dignity of all in your constitutional documents; you honor the idea by saying you are my disciples. But you do not live it. You don't welcome the poor, the powerless, or the children. I came to earth in order to bring people from the margins into the center of life. Will you not do the same?"

Every year *Fortune* magazine publishes a list of the richest Americans. It is one of the most widely quoted editions of that magazine and the list is published in hundreds of newspapers throughout the country. The popularity of this list tells us a lot about the values not only of *Fortune* magazine, but also of American culture. We measure capitalistic success by net worth. The effect of seeing someone else's net worth published makes us conscious of our own. If our net worth is up, we feel good; if it has gone down, we feel bad.

The reality of life in our culture is that personal worth or value is often equated with net worth. Though it is never explicitly said, in Western cultures the value of a person is often measured by his or her economic capacity. This philosophy is diametrically opposed to the teachings and practice of Jesus. When his disciples were speculating about greatness in the kingdom of God, Jesus used an object lesson:

> At that time the disciples came to Jesus and asked, "Who is the greatest in the kingdom of heaven?" He called a child, whom he put among them, and said, "Truly I tell you, unless you change and become like children, you will never enter the kingdom of heaven. Whoever becomes humble like this child is the greatest in the kingdom of heaven. Whoever welcomes one such child in my name welcomes me" (Matt. 18:1–5).

In the kingdom of heaven, greatness and value are measured by humility, not net worth. One of the standards is the willingness to welcome children in Jesus' name because it grants them their own dignity, their own uniqueness and value in the sight of God.

Jesus also demonstrated this in his healing. Though many examples could be given, his healing of the crippled woman (Luke 13:10–17) shows his commitment to the inherent dignity of all people. It was a Sabbath healing, and the religious leaders were indignant at Jesus for telling her, "Woman, you are set free from your ailment" (verse 13). Jesus exposed their hypocrisy with his words:

> But the Lord answered him and said, "You hypocrites! Does not each of you on the Sabbath untie his ox or his donkey from the manger, and lead it away to give it water? And ought not this woman, a daughter of Abraham whom Satan bound for eighteen long years, be set free from this bondage on the Sabbath day?" (Luke 13:15–16)

This woman was a "daughter of Abraham." She had an inherent dignity. She was more valuable than oxen and donkeys. That was the message and the action of Jesus. It is also his message to us today.

The Challenge of Race

While recognizing and embracing the dignity of all people we must deal with the issue of race or, in the politically correct language of the late twentieth century, the "challenge of diversity." The challenge of race in the United States, as well as many countries of the world, helps to bring an edge, an especially visible charge, to the idea of the dignity of all people. The current debate centers on the issue of whether race matters and should be considered in public policy and law. Should America be a color-blind society that rewards merit wherever it is found and tries to "make the playing field level" for all so that the "best" can emerge? Or should our society attempt to assure "equal opportunity" or "proportional representation"? Should race be a factor in hiring and promotion? In deciding on the propriety of voting districts? Should we be moving toward a greater philosophy of integration and inclusion in our culture, or are the forces of separatism so strong that we ought to relax the earlier quest for integration?

These questions of law and public policy only hint at a deeper issue of race—the possibility and desirability of genuine friendship across race in our culture. The issue is powerfully illustrated in the 1996 movie *A Time to Kill* which was based on the novel of the same name by John Grisham. The story begins with the rape and near murder of a ten-year-old African-American girl by two drunken young white men in a small Mississippi town. In a fit of rage, the girl's father, Carl Lee Bates, guns down the two men as they are about to appear for trial. The majority of the film then deals with the defense of Carl Lee Bates.

He secures the services of a young local white lawyer, Jake Brigance, who endures threats to his family and the burning of his home to defend Carl Lee. He tries to argue that Carl Lee was not guilty by reason of insanity. The defense effort does not go particularly well, so the night before final arguments, Brigance visits Carl Lee in his jail cell to tell him the prospects for acquittal are not good.

Brigance tells Carl Lee that because the probability of a conviction is so high, he feels as if he is letting his "friend" down. In response, Carl Lee Bates points out that Brigance had never visited—and in fact, didn't even know where Bates lived. Then he says calmly and without malice, "Let's just get one thing straight, here. *You* are the enemy." Taken aback, Brigance asks for clarification. In simple and eloquent, yet determined language, Carl Lee tells Brigance that their worlds are so far apart that they could never be friends. As a matter of fact, Carl Lee had hired Brigance precisely because Brigance understood the minds and hearts of white people. Brigance could play on their emotions, talk like they talked and reason like they reasoned. Ultimately Brigance used Carl Lee's insight to appeal to the "white mind" of the jury. Astonishingly, Carl Lee Bates is acquitted. The film closes with a scene of a victory party at the Bates home. Mingling among the African-American guests are Jake Brigance, his wife and his little daughter. Will it be possible for Jake and Carl Lee to truly become friends and feel comfortable on each other's turf? No answer is given, because the question must be answered by each of the viewers.

The movie was powerful and poignant for the two authors of this book because one of us (Glandion) is black and one

(Bill) is white; one is African-American and one European-American. We have worked together for several years, and know of no other interracial writing partnership like ours in the American-Christian world. Even so, the film made us probe our own hearts and commitments. We can see in our relationship both the promise and peril of interracial friendships in our culture.

Let us speak, for a brief moment, about our friendship. We met for the first time in the late 1960s in Menlo Park, CA, when Glandion (born 1949) came with a few other people from his church in Oakland to visit and speak to Bill's (born 1952) church youth group in Menlo Park. Glandion was nurtured in an inner-city neighborhood and came of age during the height of the Black Panther Party in Oakland. But he had already been captivated by a vision of Christian faith, and was struggling with his ambitions and his identity as a young black Christian man in the San Francisco-Oakland area during the late 1960s. Bill grew up in a Connecticut suburb of New York City and moved to Menlo Park in 1967 when his father was transferred to the San Francisco office. He made a profession of faith in Menlo Park in 1969 and was also captivated by the vision of living as a disciple of Jesus in those tumultuous times.

Our paths diverged and we did not meet again until 1990, which is the date we both consider the beginning of our friendship. Glandion was the director of InterVarsity Missions Fellowship and traveled a good deal to speak on Christian college campuses—which took him to spiritual emphasis week speaker at the college where Bill taught. We ate lunch together and saw something in each other that captivated and attracted us. For Bill it was Glandion's enormous spiritual sensitivity, his passionate heart, his instinctive sense of the spiritual yearnings of people. For Glandion it was Bill's intelligence, spirit, and energy. For the first several months, and even years, of our friendship, we realized how similarly our minds worked, whether understanding the spiritual yearnings of our culture or applying particular passages of Scripture to our lives. We would call each other regularly to plan projects or to speak about everything and nothing.

Our lives have changed since 1990, and those changes have brought challenges to our friendship. We have both experienced changes in location, in work, and in our desires to explore long-ignored or forgotten areas from our past. Some of the changes in the last several years may have resulted from a continuing restlessness that we thought would go away after we reached the supposedly safe haven of early middle age and growing families.

The bond that ties us, that keeps us coming back to each other despite our cultural and experiential differences, is a bond forged in faith. Yet our faith continues to grow as we try to understand and support each other's struggles in life. For example, we have both struggled with our *past*. The older we get, the more we realize that we are, at the same instant, free *and* bound, individuals *and* products of communities, able to choose *and* limited by our choices, blessed *and* marked by the experiences of the past. We have explored our family roots, whether that means speaking with aging parents about decisions that were made thirty years ago, or collecting historical records about ancestors who lived more than 200 years ago. Coming to grips with our past is a necessary part of understanding our present. We have discovered that we need to take the time to do this patient "research." The data is there, and some of it is relatively easy to find.

We have discovered that when we look at our past, the pain and the promise of life become more clearly defined. We see the losses of our families, their premature losses of energy, love and life—the "quiet desperation," as Thoreau calls it, of living. But we also discover special gifts of grace in a keepsake, a notebook, an old letter, a story that had never sunk into our consciousness. The tears we shed are tears of recognition and belonging, of coming home and realizing that we are bound to others with a cord more indestructible than the strongest steel alloy.

Struggling with our past lends stability to the present. It helps us see that we are part of the vast tapestry of life, a tapestry that tells a story as significant in its own way as the Bayeux tapestry tells of the crossing of the English Channel by William the Conqueror and his victory at Hastings over the forces of Harold Godwinson in 1066. We affirm each other in our struggles with the past, and our admiration for each other grows as we discover previous pains, joys, and bits of information that have contributed to making us who we are.

There has also been the struggle of *call*. We were led to believe while growing up that the greatest time of personal turmoil we would face would come in our teens and early twenties, as we were trying to "separate" from our families and forge our unique identities. After we navigated those perilous waters and had "settled down," we were told, life would have a predictable character to it, a character we would eagerly embrace. "Settling down" meant getting married, having a family, purchasing a house and finding stable employment which would reward us with steadily increasing responsibility and salary as we got older.

Not! Our experience has defied the pleasant mythology of our parents, shaped in the wake of the Great Depression and World War II. The most significant area where this myth has been challenged is in the area of vocation or, in theological terms, in our sense of call. We have struggled to "match" our sense of call with a particular job location that would bring the satisfaction, challenge and remuneration we were told to expect. At times we stand back in awe when we see people move through life seemingly effortlessly, with clear vocational goals, loving families, kids with straight teeth and straight A's. We wonder if we simply are demanding too much out of life. But at other times we are deeply grateful for the vocational uncertainties of our lives, and recognize they are used by the Spirit of God to provide insights that a "stable" vocational life might not yield.

Our friendship has held together, also, despite the struggles of our individual *spiritual quests*. Perhaps because of our "vocational flexibility," we have become more open to the varied nature of the Christian life and the search for spirituality. We are both products of the Reformed theological tradition of Protestantism, which traces its origin to Calvin's Geneva in the sixteenth century and was refracted through the two lenses of seventeenth century Dutch Calvinism and English Puritanism. The Reformed tradition has always stressed the importance of the Christian mind and a thoughtful consideration of faith. Both of us are happy to be products of such a tradition.

Yet we have discovered that this tradition isn't enough to satisfy some of our restless spiritual yearnings. We have explored the spiritual practices of other traditions of the Christian family (especially Catholic spirituality) and have become increasingly open to learning from other religious traditions (such as Judaism or Buddhism) whose insights into spiritual practices such as prayer and meditation can nurture us. In addition, our spiritual quest has led us into new fields of investigation such as art history and law—and will probably open new vistas in the future that we cannot yet imagine.

All of these struggles have gone on during the past seven or eight years as we have developed our friendship. At times our conversations have flowed with all the freshness and power of a mountain stream after the winter snow melt. At times, we have strained to hear the pain in each other's voice. Yet our friendship continues, despite personal changes, distance and larger cultural forces working against interracial friendship.

If Jesus were in the flesh today, we think he would say, "Learn to welcome each other, to befriend each other and to honor those of different races. For it may be the outsider, the one *not* in your group, who is favored by God." Jesus showed the truth of this many times in his ministry. It is most apparent in his dealings with and references to the Samaritans.

The Samaritans lived between Galilee and Judea, and were considered half-Jews because of their supposed descent from some of the ten tribes of Israel deported to Assyria during the conquest of Israel in 722 B.C. In many communities concerned with purity of religion, "half-breeds" are treated worse than complete outsiders. So it was for Samaritans. A pious Jew making the 100-mile trip from Galilee to Jerusalem would often avoid the direct route (through Samaria) in favor of crossing the Jordan, going across the Jordanian plain, and then coming back into the Promised Land near Jericho. It was very inconvenient, but many people took the detour to avoid making contact with the Samaritans.

Three instances in the Gospels highlight the spiritual sensitivity and compassion of the Samaritans. The most obvious, the Parable of the Good Samaritan (Luke 10:29–37), describes a Samaritan coming to the aid of a badly injured person and taking care of his needs. The Samaritan proves himself to be a better neighbor than the Jewish religious leaders. Later in the Gospel of Luke is the story of Jesus healing ten lepers (Luke 17:11–19). The only leper who came back to thank Jesus was a Samaritan. As if to highlight how incongruous this would be to Jewish ears, Jesus says:

> Were not ten made clean? But the other nine, where are they? Was none of them found to return and give praise to God except this foreigner? (verses 17–18)

It was the despised foreigner, the invisible person who was most grateful and was commended by Jesus.

Finally, there is the story of Jesus and the Samaritan woman (John 4). Jesus, tired from a long day walking, sat at a well in Samaria and asked a Samaritan woman for a drink of water. She was taken aback because he, a Jewish male, was breaking the social code by initiating a conversation with her. As the conversation unfolded and Jesus led her to a knowledge of himself, she became the first Christian missionary by going home to tell her townspeople about him.

Jesus' conduct sends the message that the Gospel is not to be limited only to our own ethnic community, racial group or those with similar economic capacity. Let there be no mistake, though. The development of friendship across cultures or races is difficult. We constantly have to keep before us our focus, our center, our Christ.

The Snare of Greed

As we continue to deal with the inherent dignity of all people and the challenge of race, we must also beware the snare of greed. Take a look at this quote from *Harper's* Magazine:

> It is a stock remark that Americans love the dollar. The saying, like most stock sayings, misses the point; the real point is, not that Americans love money more than other people, but that they love *comparatively few things besides money.*

The date of this quote might surprise you: November, 1880! The writer was referring to the enterprising and greedy spirit of America in the post–Civil War period. Yet the quotation remains provocative because the root of the affections of many Americans continues to be the near-exclusive love of money.

I am not an economist, but I could list a number of factors proving that America's love affair with money continues unabated. The subtle way that money works in our lives is to convert things we once considered *wants* into *absolute needs.* Two illustrations will make this point clear.

I currently live in a neighborhood in which the homes were built between 1930 and 1940. It is a classic neighborhood with large elm trees, sidewalks and even some bricked streets. All of the old homes have garages, but they are all one- or two-car garages. The reality of life at the end of the twentieth century is that most of my neighbors own three, four or five cars. Consequently, cars are parked all over my neighborhood, in driveways and garages, on lawns and curbs. When asked about all their cars, my neighbors say they *must* have them. A car for each driver is now considered a necessity of life.

A second story involves my association with colleges. In 1970 I flew from San Francisco to New York and was driven by my grandparents to Rhode Island, where I attended Brown University. I took one trunk and one suitcase which contained everything I thought I would need. Now, when students show up at college for freshman orientation, it is not unusual to see U-Haul trucks and trailers. Dormitory rooms have had to be rewired to accommodate our growing need for electrical power. I do not think of myself as opposed to technology or attempts to make life more comfortable; indeed, I welcome many new developments. The point is, however, that what once were wants have become needs. And the trend shows no signs of stopping.

In 1995 a major brokerage house in New York came out with advice for "Baby Boomer and Generation X" families, informing them how many assets they must have by age 65 in order to live comfortably in retirement. The figure? $1.5 million. Such a figure sends a shudder through parents trying to figure out how to pay for their children's college tuition, much less how to live comfortably for the twenty, thirty or even forty years after retirement which may someday be the norm.

In 1995 the U.S. stock markets performed at unprecedented levels. The Dow Jones Industrial average increased more than 25 percent and the NASDAQ more than 35 percent. Select stocks and mutual funds performed even better, and the markets have been climbing steadily ever since. The observation I made during the frenzy of 1995 and 1996, while the numbers were rising with vertiginous rapidity, is that more money actually *excited greed* in people rather than *satisfied* their longings for financial security.

But I realize this mentality is nothing new. Jesus often spoke directly about money and greed. One time someone in the crowd asked Jesus to divide the family inheritance among the children. Let us examine his response:

> But [Jesus] said to him, "Friend, who set me to be a judge or arbitrator over you?" And he said to them, "Take care! Be on your guard against all kinds of greed; for one's life does not consist in the abundance of possessions." Then he told them a parable: "The land of a rich man produced abundantly. And he thought to himself, 'What should I do, for I have no place to store my crops?' Then he said, 'I will do this: I will pull down my barns and build larger ones, and there I will store all my grain and my goods. And I will say to my soul, 'Soul, you have ample goods laid up for many years; relax, eat, drink, be

merry.' But God said to him, 'You fool! This very night your life is being demanded of you. And the things you have prepared, whose will they be?' So it is with those who store up treasures for themselves but are not rich toward God" (Luke 12:14–21).

The rich man in Jesus' parable might have been the world's first financial planner. He had a good harvest; he wanted to ensure his financial security; he built bigger barns; he expected to live off his labor and his investments (which is the goal of many people today). What was the result? God called him a fool. But why would a person who seems, by our standards, to be acting prudently, be called a fool?

Jesus understood deeply that money concerns weaken one's interest in things of God and, indirectly, in one's concern for being a neighbor. Those who have money spend time worrying about how to keep or increase it. Their view of what is good for society is almost always colored by how it will affect their asset level. In this way, riches can make one as blind as the beggar Bartimaeus, as lame as the man seated by the pool of Bethzatha. The type of person whom we might admire or reward is called a fool by Jesus. There doesn't appear, at first glance, to be an easy way to reconcile the two value systems.

Living from the Heart

Our closing thoughts will be not a prohibition, but a word of encouragement, something that stresses the joys of life rather than its dangers. I call it *living from the heart, living in freedom,* or *living with joy.* Jesus said that life does not consist of the abundance of possessions, but the abundance of the heart. The heart is the source of life, the fountainhead of both good and evil, the key to life. Mastery of the things of the heart is the crucial issue of life. Jesus' promise of abundant life to his followers (John 10:10) retains its validity today.

But in what does abundant life consist? What does it mean to live from the heart? What is the abundance which Jesus promises and how does one tap into it? Many Christians do not think of their lives as abundant or even potentially abundant. Our reality is more frequently described with words such as "painful," "confused," or "bored." Indeed, much of life is painful; often we are confused; sometimes boredom cannot be avoided. I think the key to living the abundant life is learning to live with pain. In developing a strategy of how to live with pain, I will suggest two things: living with gratitude, and saying "yes" to today.

Pain is a part of so many lives and comes in numerous diverse forms. It includes physical ailments and limitations as well as mental, psychological and spiritual scars we accumulate throughout life. Pain is one of the most demanding taskmasters we will ever encounter. It is more insistent than an unsympathetic boss, more unrelenting than the summer sun, more unforgiving than a personal enemy. Pain is a force that wants to rule our lives and is not satisfied until it has rendered us helpless in its grasp.

The key to abundant living is developing a strategy to live with pain, so that life rather than pain has the last word. In Reynolds Price's book, *A Whole New Life,* quoted previously, he talks about the reality of pain that devastated him between 1984 and 1988, and the way he has learned to live with constant pain since then as a paraplegic. His approach to pain is one that needs to be heard. He says:

> From long reading in the lives of others less lucky than I, and from years of watching not only myself but a few close friends in agony, I think I can say that almost any degree of physical pain can be borne. And not only borne but literally displaced from the actual center of a human life and then ignored. I can make that claim because I'm convinced that all pain has one huge design on us—to rule our minds—and therefore the secret of living with pain is wanting hard to throw it out of central control, then finding the sane means to work that steady mental combination of distancing and coexistence (p. 160).

The crucial phrase in this quotation is to "throw it (pain) out of central control." Throwing pain out of central control is a decision of the mind. At times it also requires the use of medication or other professional treatment, but the key is beginning with a mental decision that the pain will no longer have central place. Do not be deceived about the difficulty of such a decision and how often it needs to be reaffirmed. It may very well be the most difficult decision of a person's life. Let me give another illustration.

One of the only professional sports I watch with any regularity is basketball. I enjoy seeing the speed, strength and elegance of the athletes. I have learned to look for lessons of life that come through that sport. The first lesson is that you have to live with constant distractions and small acts of injustice. Basketball is a game of numerous fouls, only a few of which are actually called by the officials. It teaches me that life is filled with distractions and injustices, only a few of which are noticed and compensated with a foul shot. One has to learn to keep playing in spite of unfairness and inconvenience.

Another lesson is that even after you have made a fantastic move and scored a stunning basket, you need to hurry back into a defensive position. You cannot rest on your laurels or gloat over your skill. If you do, your opponent will score two points at the other end and negate the effects of your arresting play. But the lesson from basketball most important for this section is that the best players in the world are those who have learned to play with pain. They play with taped ankles, bandaged thighs, oversized goggles to protect injured eyes, strained muscles, broken noses and a host of other ailments that very few people can even imagine. It is a mental and physical struggle to play. Sometimes the injuries are bad enough to keep a player out of a few games, but the goal is always to return to the fray as quickly as possible. Pain cannot become the central reality of life for a professional basketball player; winning must be.

The same is true of us. To live from the heart means that each of us, in the secret depths of his or her heart, must learn to live with pain in such a way that it does not master us. We need to live so that the sweetly alluring voice of pain does not turn us into bitter, angry, grief-stricken, pessimistic and destructive people. We dare not become discouraged and surrender. Pain often wins the battle because it is such a formidable foe, such an unrelenting adversary. But we can win the war if we don't give up.

A Heart of Gratitude

One of my favorite poems is by the twentieth century American poet e. e. cummings. By ignoring rules of capitalization and punctuation in his poetry, he forces the reader to take it slowly and let the words seep into every pore of the person's existence. My favorite poem is called "i thank You God," and the first stanza is as follows:

i thank You God for most this amazing
day: for the leaping greenly spirits of trees
and a blue true dream of sky; and for everything
which is natural which is infinite which is yes

The key to abundant living is learning to greet each day and live it with a grateful heart. Gratitude must sing and smile. It sings without inhibition, "When morning gilds the skies, my heart awaking cries, 'May Jesus Christ be praised!'" It smiles at the opening of a flower, the cry of a baby, the countless surprises of life which it chooses to perceive as grace rather than as interruptions or distractions.

The grateful heart is a praying heart, which reflects its spirit to God—sometimes loudly and sometimes silently. It says, "I praise you, worship you, adore you, God. You hold the heavens in your hands and all the stars rejoice in your glory. You come in the sunrise and the song of the morn, and you bless the splendor of the noonday."

When Jesus healed the ten lepers (Luke 17:11–19), only one of them turned back to praise God and thank Jesus. He, the Samaritan, became an object lesson for Jesus on the proper way to respond to the touch of God in one's life. From the beginning to the end of the Scripture, it is the gratitude of the people of God which leads to abundance. The complaints of the people of Israel in the wilderness brought death and dissension; their gratitude for the work of God among them led to prosperity. The psalmist captures the biblical spirit best when he says:

> What shall I return to the Lord for all his bounty to me?
> I will lift up the cup of salvation and call on the name of the
>   Lord, . . .
> I will offer to you a thanksgiving sacrifice and call on the
>   name of the Lord
> (Psalm 116:12–13, 17).

Saying "Yes" to Today

The seventeenth-century French philosopher and mathematician, Blaise Pascal, lamented that one of the hazards of living is that we humans tend either to live in the past or the future and never in the present. We either regret or glorify the past, and we long for or dread what the future may hold. In the meantime, life today passes us by. We do not enjoy the joys of the moment because of our obsession with the past or the future.

The importance of saying "yes" to today and the consequences of not doing so is a theme of the book *Terry* by former U.S. Senator and Democratic presidential nominee, George McGovern. His third child, Terry, was found December 13, 1994, frozen to death in the snow in an alley in Madison, Wisconsin. McGovern's book is the story of her life, her winning and loving personality and her struggle with her "twin demons," depression and alcoholism. He tells how the loss of a child leaves an almost unbearable weight of grief and a yawning emptiness in the lives of parents and siblings. He describes the guilt he still feels over Terry. He searches his past for some clues that may have contributed to Terry's condition. His questions are the same as our would be: Was I so concerned with my own career and aspirations that I wasn't a good father? Did I miss signs in our family history that she would have been susceptible to alcoholism and depression? Did we really do all we could in the last six months of her life to provide the support she needed?

When all is said and done, however, George McGovern gets to the nub of what he believes would have helped his daughter:

> As I have learned more of Terry's life, I have come to a deepening conclusion that she was at her best when she was conscientiously involved with the AA Twelve Step Program—focusing on staying sober and recovering from alcoholism one day at a time. She was at her worst when, sometimes stimulated by psychologists, she looked backward in self-pity to the injured child suffering from the perceived misdeeds and ignorance of others. It is inevitable that all of us are affected in the present by our personal history. We may need to understand that history before we can fully cope with our current personal problems. But it is hazardous and, I believe, counterproductive to become frozen in time by an obsession with past wrongs and errors. At times, Terry seemed incapable of moving forward because of her preoccupations with her memories and perceptions of the past (pp. 127–128).

We, too, become "frozen in time" whenever we believe that the past has already spoken the last word on our lives, when we can no longer see the joy of today, when we seek to blame others for our condition in life.

To say "yes" to today means we receive life as a gift of God, and accept responsibility as stewards of that gift for a little time.

When all is said and done, when we work hard and suffer hard, when we mingle our transient joys with deep losses, when we try to untangle, and fail to untangle, the complex web of our past, we can turn ourselves back to the living Christ and say "yes" to him again. There is no other satisfactory way to live.

Let me leave you with a final challenge from the psalms:

O that today you would listen to [God's] voice!

Do not harden your hearts, as at Meribah,
as on the day at Massah in the wilderness (95:7–8).

Today is the day to listen to Christ's voice. Let your hearts
burn and your minds yearn. You will rediscover that Christ
still calls us to his table, that he breaks bread with us, that he
gives himself to us, and that his presence goes with us to the
end of our days.

⌒ •

Lord Jesus I began asking that you would burn within my soul, burn
within my spirit, and burn within my heart. Set within me a flame,
a passion to be a person of integrity. To follow you and to deeply love
you. Help me to expand my understandings of the scriptures and
prayer. Help me to know truth in community and help me to experience the deeper moments of reflection upon the cross and suffering. I want to be like Jesus in my heart, in my heart. Lord I want to
be like Jesus in my heart. Thank you Jesus that your spirituality has
touched mine. That I see within you integrity, love, and commitment. I know I need that in my own life. Thank you that you have
become closer to me through my pursuing and understanding you,
your humanity, and in your love. Thank you lord Jesus, burn within
me, be within me. In your name. Amen.

BIBLIOGRAPHY

Chapter 1

Thompson, Marjorie J., *Soul Feast: An Invitation to the Christian Spiritual Life* (Louisville: Westminster John Knox, 1995).

Chapter 3

Maclean, Norman, *Young Men and Fire* (Chicago: University of Chicago, 1991).

Chapter 4

Norris, Kathleen, *The Cloister Walk* (New York: Riverhead Books, 1996).

Chapter 5

Borg, Marcus J., *Meeting Jesus Again for the First Time* (San Francisco: Harper San Francisco, 1994), especially, ch. 3.

Chapter 6

Halberstam, David, *The Powers That Be* (New York: Alfred A. Knopf, 1979).
Styron, William, *Darkness Visible: A Memoir of Madness* (New York: Random House, 1990).
Broyard, Anatole, *Intoxicated by My Illness and Other Writings on Life and Death* (New York: Clarkson Potter, 1992).

Chapter 7

King, Martin Luther, Jr., "Letter from Birmingham City Jail," in *A Testament of Hope: The Essential Writings of Martin Luther King, Jr.*, edited by James Melvin Washington (San Francisco: Harper and Row, 1986), 289–302.

Chapter 8

Jackson, Phil and Hugh Delehanty, *Sacred Hoops: Spiritual Lessons of a Hardwood Warrior* (New York: Hyperion, 1995).

Chapter 9

Price, Reynolds, *A Whole New Life: An Illness and a Healing* (New York: Plume Books, 1994).

Lane, William L., *Commentary on the Gospel of Mark* (Grand Rapids: Eerdmans, 1974).

Chapter 10

McGovern, George, *Terry: My Daughter's Life-and-Death Struggle with Alcoholism* (New York: Random House, 1996).

Subject Index

SCRIPTURE INDEX

17:11–19 214, 220
17:17–18 214
18:1–8 91
18:11 195
18:22 150
18:24 150
19:1–10 151
19:7 149
19:9 151
20:20–26 152
20:25 152
20:27–40 70
22:40–41 82
23:46 114
24 45
24:13–24 28
24:13–35 19, 28
24:21 29, 30
24:25 30
24:25–27 29
24:28–31 30
24:31 31
24:32 32
24:33–35
24:45 59

John

1:41 123
1:42 123
1:45 123

1:47 85, 123
1:48 123
1:49 123
2:4 113
2:24 175
5:6 124
6:68 177
7:6 113
8:31–32 34
10:10 217
10:38 176
13:1 113
13–17 175
13:35 176
14:11 176
14:12 178
14:20 176
14:23 176
15 177
15:1–2 177
15:4–10 177
15:5 177
15:7 89, 178
15:16 39
16:23–24 89
16:33 179
19:25–27 45
20 45

Acts

1:6 47

Romans

5:3–5 184
8:22 125

1 Corinthians

6:19–20 39

2 Corinthians

3:18 94
5:17 167

Galatians

5:22–23 178

Hebrews

1:13 74

1Peter

1:6–7 49

James

2–4 48–49

The Talmud

Yoma 8.6—Mishnah
  102

Glandion Carney was founder and pastor of the Centerpoint Community of Spiritual Formation in Grand Rapids, Michigan. He is now urban missions pastor for Briarwood Presbyterian Church in Birmingham, Alabama. **William Long,** who formerly taught history and government at Sterling College, is studying for his law degree at the Willamette University College in Salem, Oregon. They are also coauthors of *Longing for God* and *Trusting God Again.*